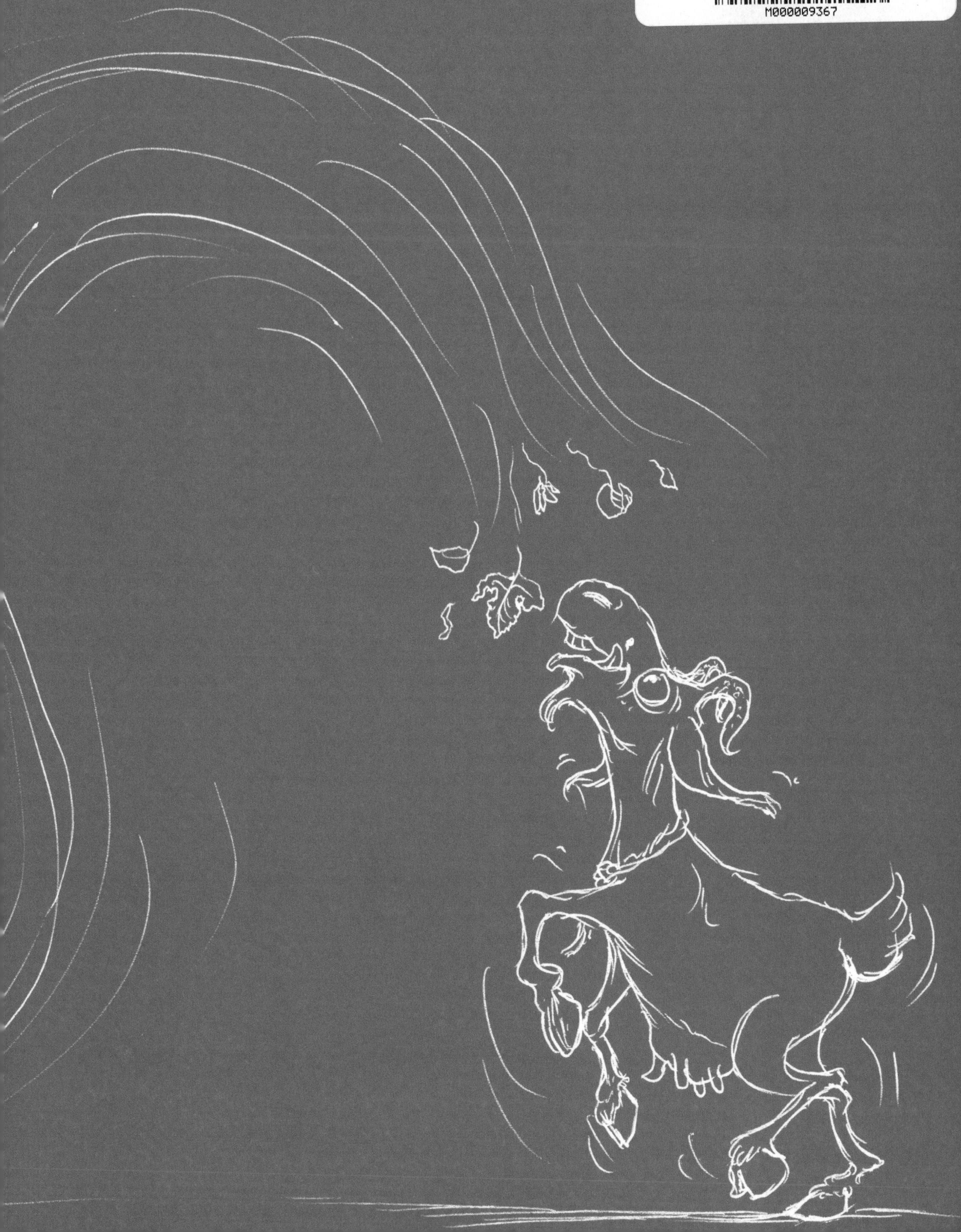

From Foe to Friend & Other Stories
by S.Y. Agnon

A Graphic Novel by Shay Charka

In memory of my grandfather
Moshe Yudkovitch ז״ל
Dealing with Agnon reminds me of him.

FROM FOE TO FRIEND

& OTHER STORIES

by S.Y. Agnon

A Graphic Novel by Shay Charka

English language edition adapted by Jeffrey Saks

Toby

From Foe to Friend & Other Stories
by S.Y. Agnon
A Graphic Novel by Shay Charka

S.Y. Agnon Library Series Editor: Jeffrey Saks
English edition layout and design: Tani Bayer

Originally published in Hebrew as
Shay veAgnon: Sheloshah Sippurim by Schocken Publishing House Ltd., Tel Aviv (© 2012).
The English texts of the stories in this book have been adapted from the following translations of Agnon's writing: "From Foe to Friend" translated by Joel Blocker in *The Reconstructionist* (May 15, 1959); in Hebrew as *"MeOyev leOhev"* in *Elu veElu*. "Fable of the Goat" translated by Barney Rubin in: *A Book That Was Lost* (© *The* Toby Press); in Hebrew as *"Ma'aseh HaEz"* in *Elu veElu*. "The Architect and the Emperor" translated by Hillel Halkin in *To This Day* (© *The* Toby Press); in Hebrew the story appears, in passing, as part of chapter 5 in Agnon's novel *Ad Henah*.

Thanks to Shari Dash Greenspan and Debbie Herman for editorial assistance.

The Toby Press LLC
POB 8531, New Milford, CT 06776–8531, USA
& POB 2455, London W1A 5WY, ENGLAND
www.tobypress.com

This is a work of fiction. The characters, incidents, and dialogues are products of the imaginations of the author and illustrator and are not to be construed as real.

ISBN 978-1-59264-395-0

Printed and bound in the United States

FROM FOE TO FRIEND

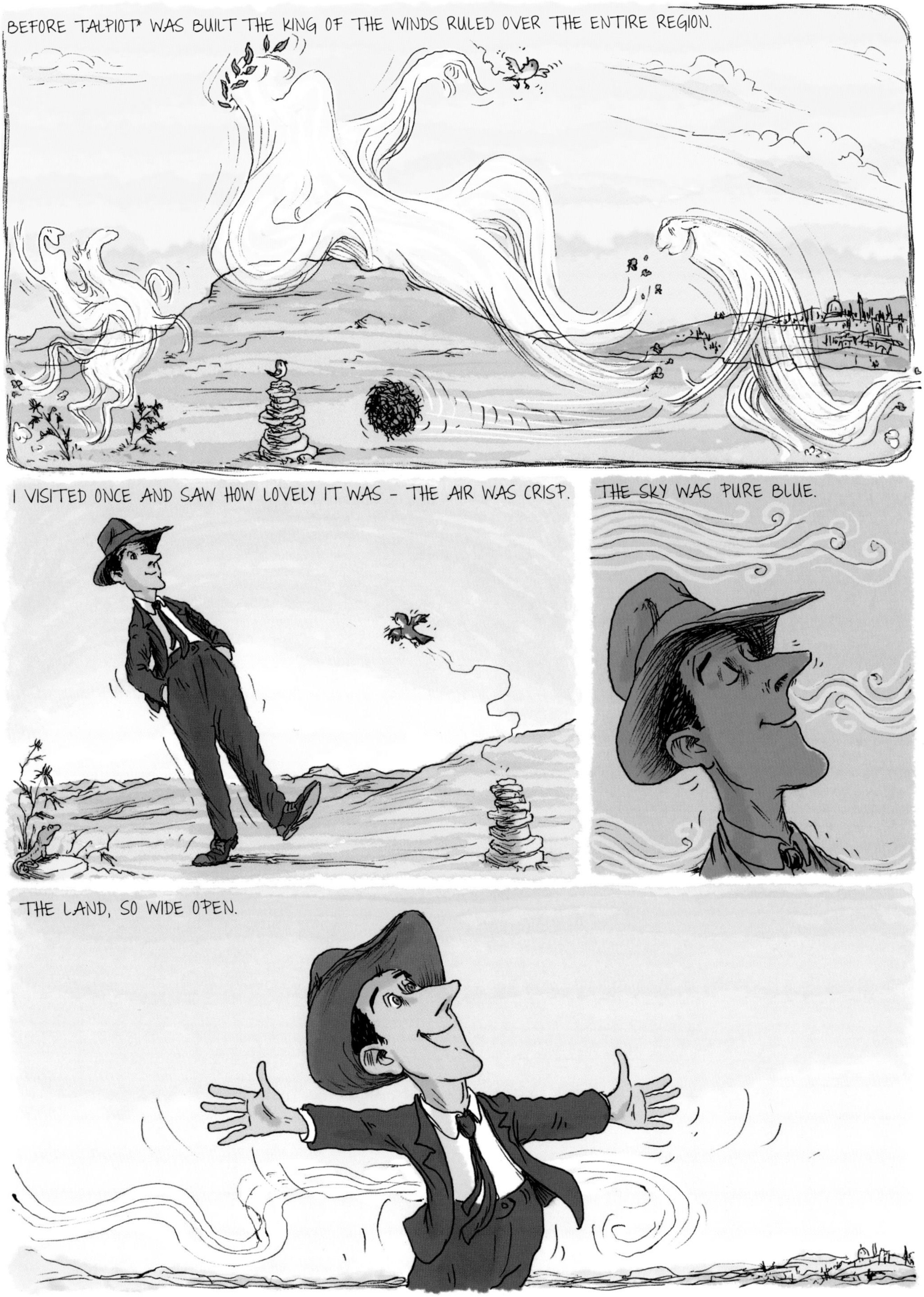
BEFORE TALPIOT* WAS BUILT THE KING OF THE WINDS RULED OVER THE ENTIRE REGION.
I VISITED ONCE AND SAW HOW LOVELY IT WAS - THE AIR WAS CRISP.
THE SKY WAS PURE BLUE.
THE LAND, SO WIDE OPEN.

* TALPIOT IS A SUBURB IN THE HILLS TO THE SOUTH OF THE OLD CITY OF JERUSALEM.

I STROLLED AROUND A BIT. THE WIND HARASSED ME.

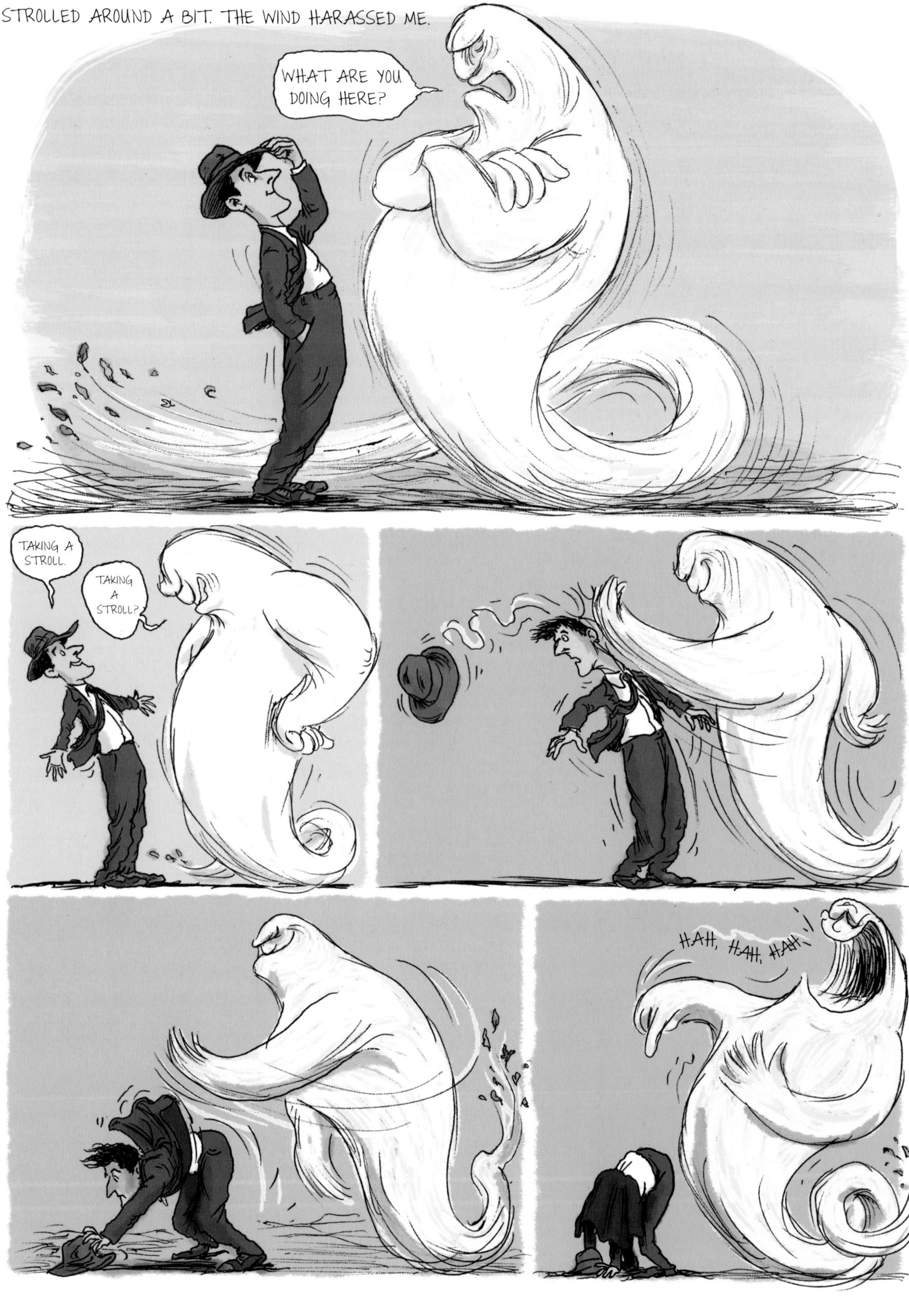
WHAT ARE YOU DOING HERE?
TAKING A STROLL.
TAKING A STROLL?
HAH, HAH, HAH

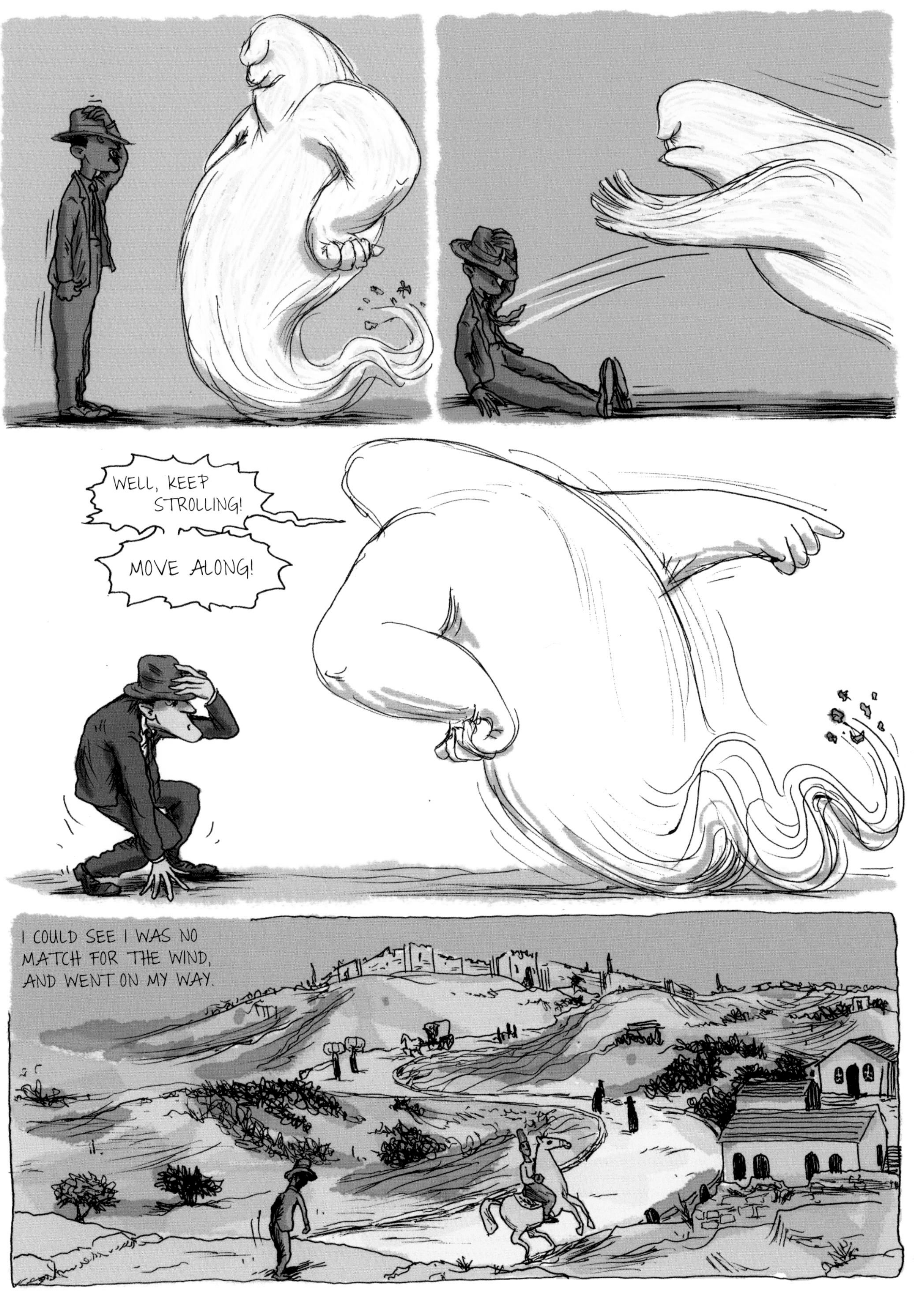
WELL, KEEP STROLLING!
MOVE ALONG!
I COULD SEE I WAS NO MATCH FOR THE WIND, AND WENT ON MY WAY.

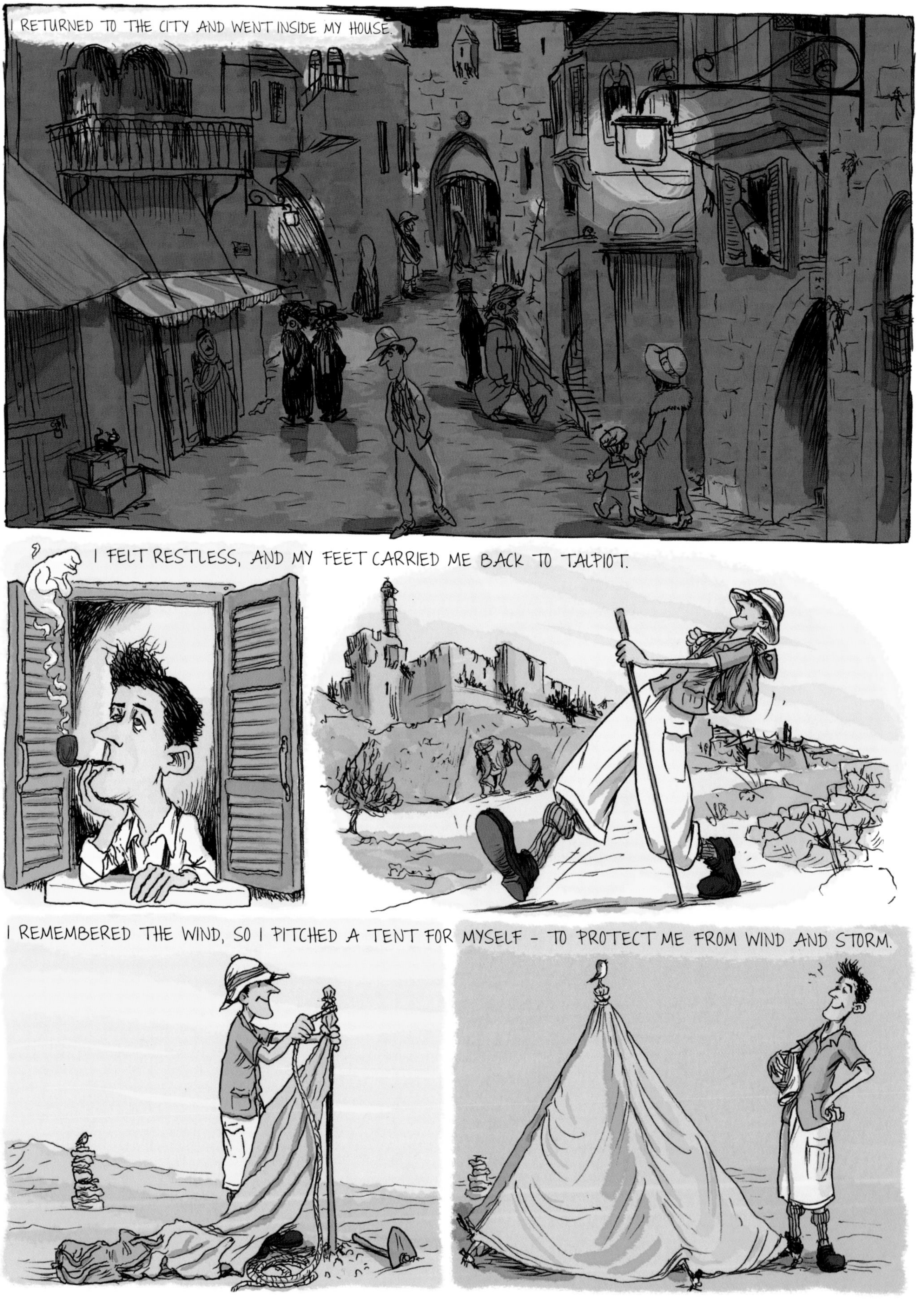
I RETURNED TO THE CITY AND WENT INSIDE MY HOUSE.
I FELT RESTLESS, AND MY FEET CARRIED ME BACK TO TALPIOT.
I REMEMBERED THE WIND, SO I PITCHED A TENT FOR MYSELF - TO PROTECT ME FROM WIND AND STORM.

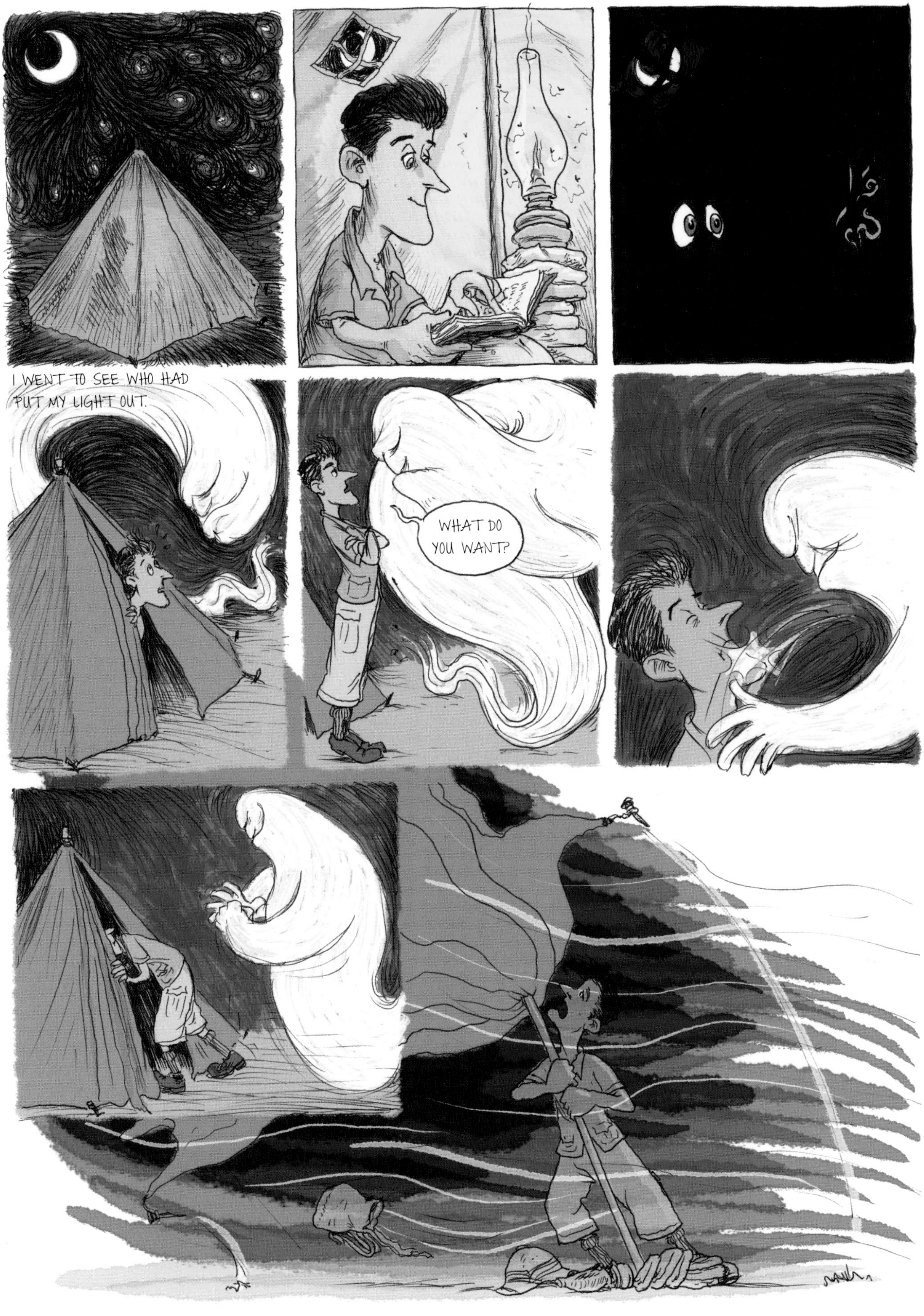
I WENT TO SEE WHO HAD PUT MY LIGHT OUT.
WHAT DO YOU WANT?

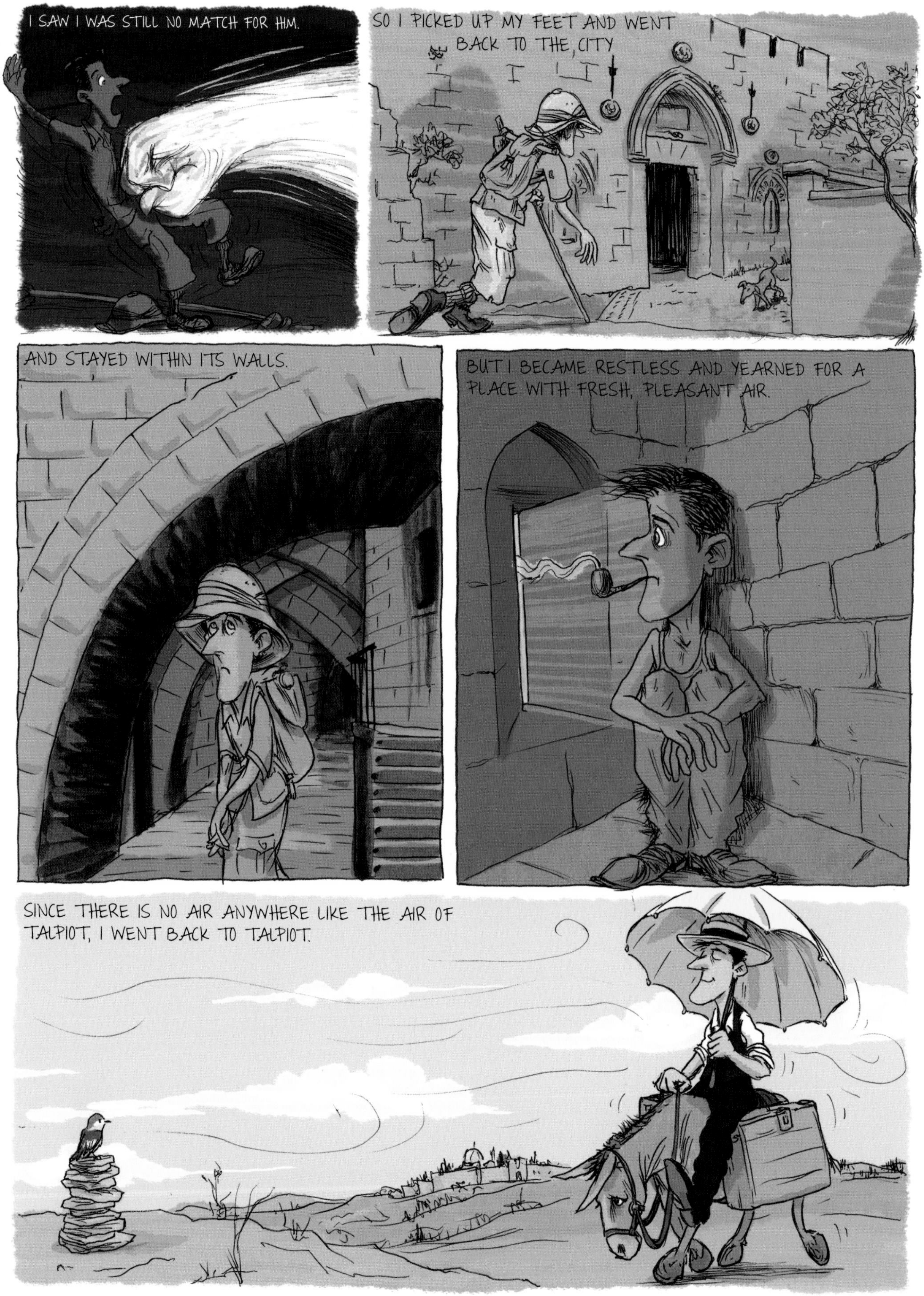
I SAW I WAS STILL NO MATCH FOR HIM.
SO I PICKED UP MY FEET AND WENT BACK TO THE CITY
AND STAYED WITHIN ITS WALLS.
BUT I BECAME RESTLESS AND YEARNED FOR A PLACE WITH FRESH, PLEASANT AIR.
SINCE THERE IS NO AIR ANYWHERE LIKE THE AIR OF TALPIOT, I WENT BACK TO TALPIOT.

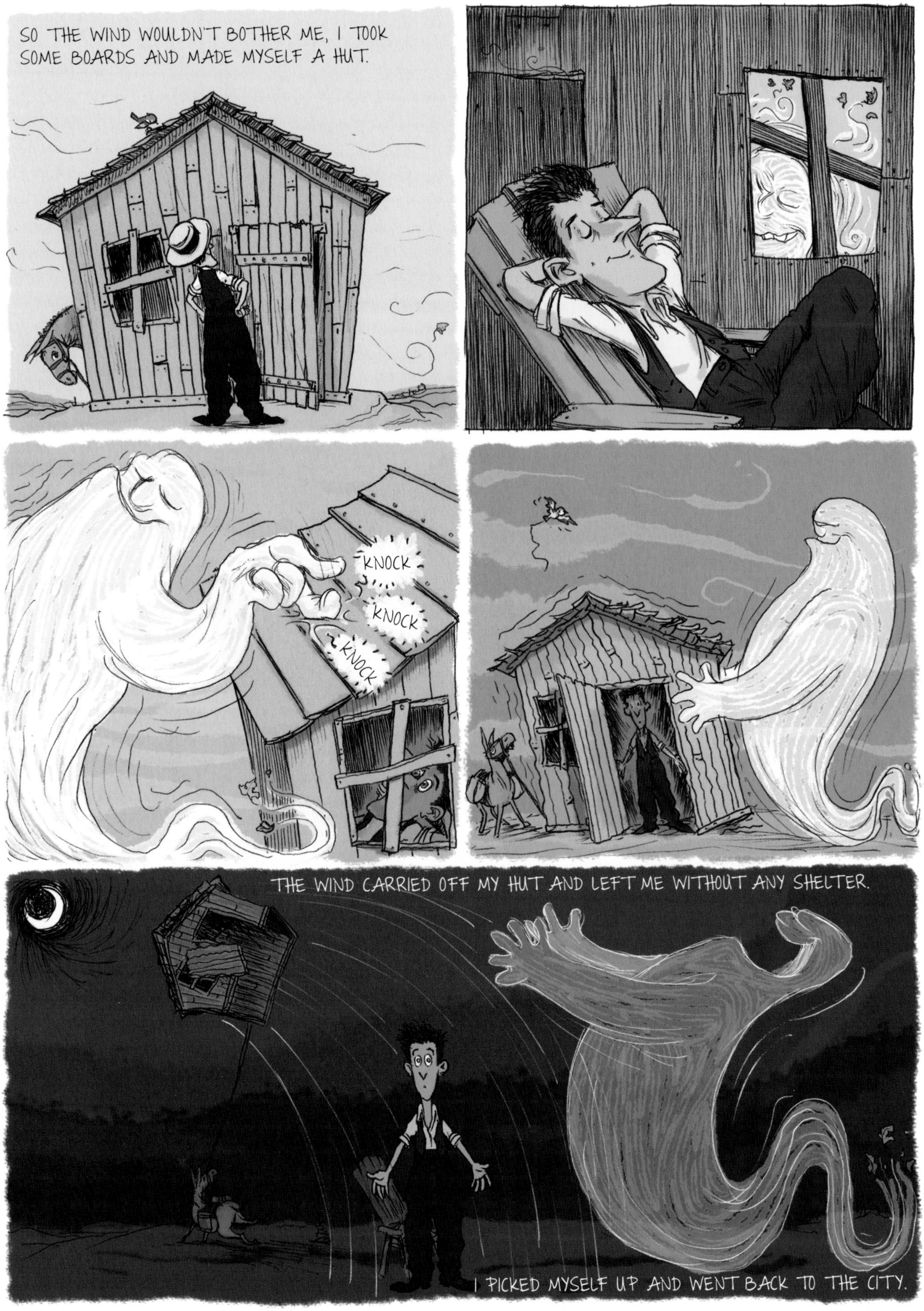
SO THE WIND WOULDN'T BOTHER ME, I TOOK SOME BOARDS AND MADE MYSELF A HUT.
KNOCK
KNOCK
KNOCK
THE WIND CARRIED OFF MY HUT AND LEFT ME WITHOUT ANY SHELTER.
I PICKED MYSELF UP AND WENT BACK TO THE CITY.

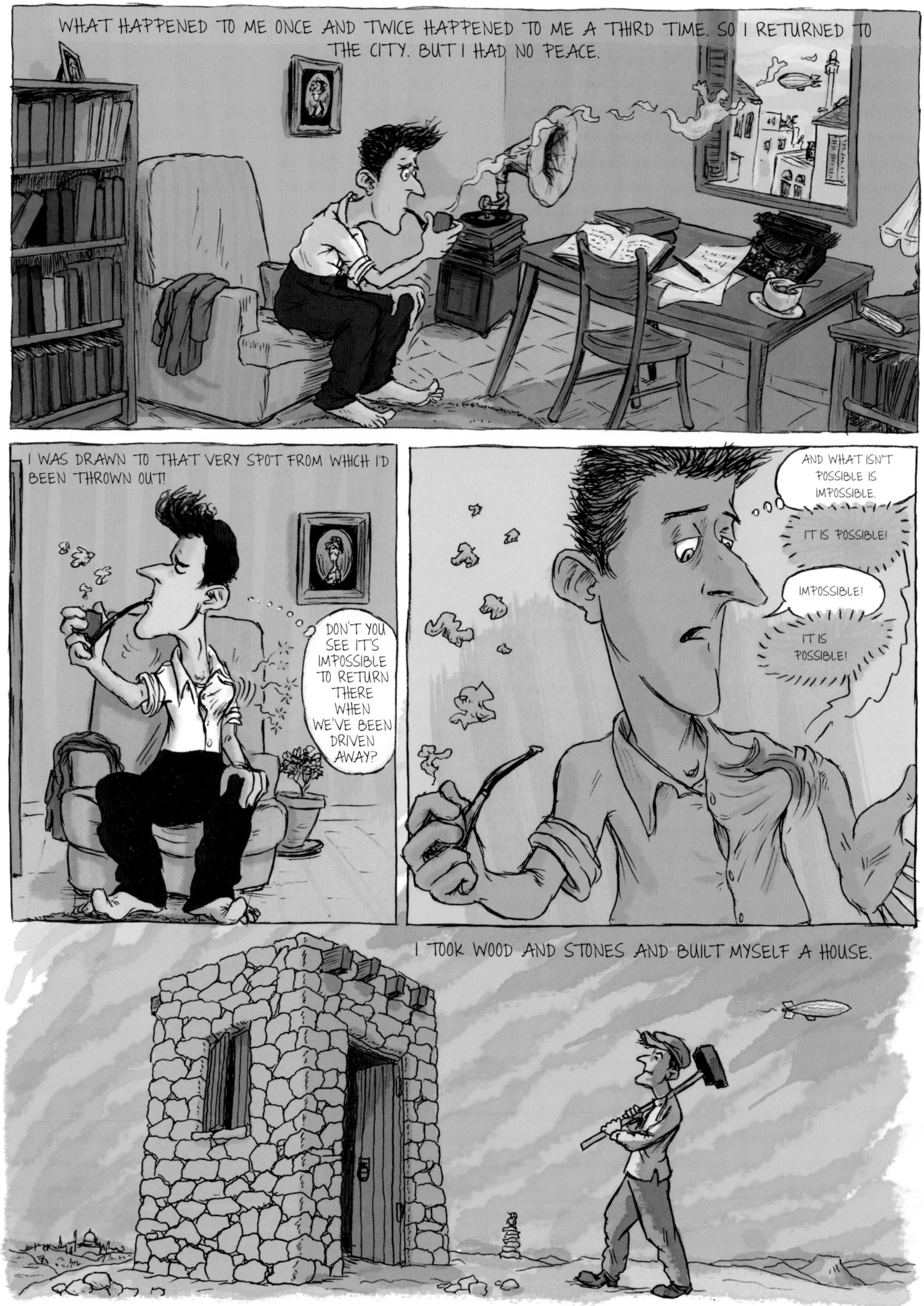
WHAT HAPPENED TO ME ONCE AND TWICE HAPPENED TO ME A THIRD TIME. SO I RETURNED TO THE CITY. BUT I HAD NO PEACE.
I WAS DRAWN TO THAT VERY SPOT FROM WHICH I'D BEEN THROWN OUT!
DON'T YOU SEE IT'S IMPOSSIBLE TO RETURN THERE WHEN WE'VE BEEN DRIVEN AWAY?
AND WHAT ISN'T POSSIBLE IS IMPOSSIBLE.
IT IS POSSIBLE!
IMPOSSIBLE!
IT IS POSSIBLE!
I TOOK WOOD AND STONES AND BUILT MYSELF A HOUSE.

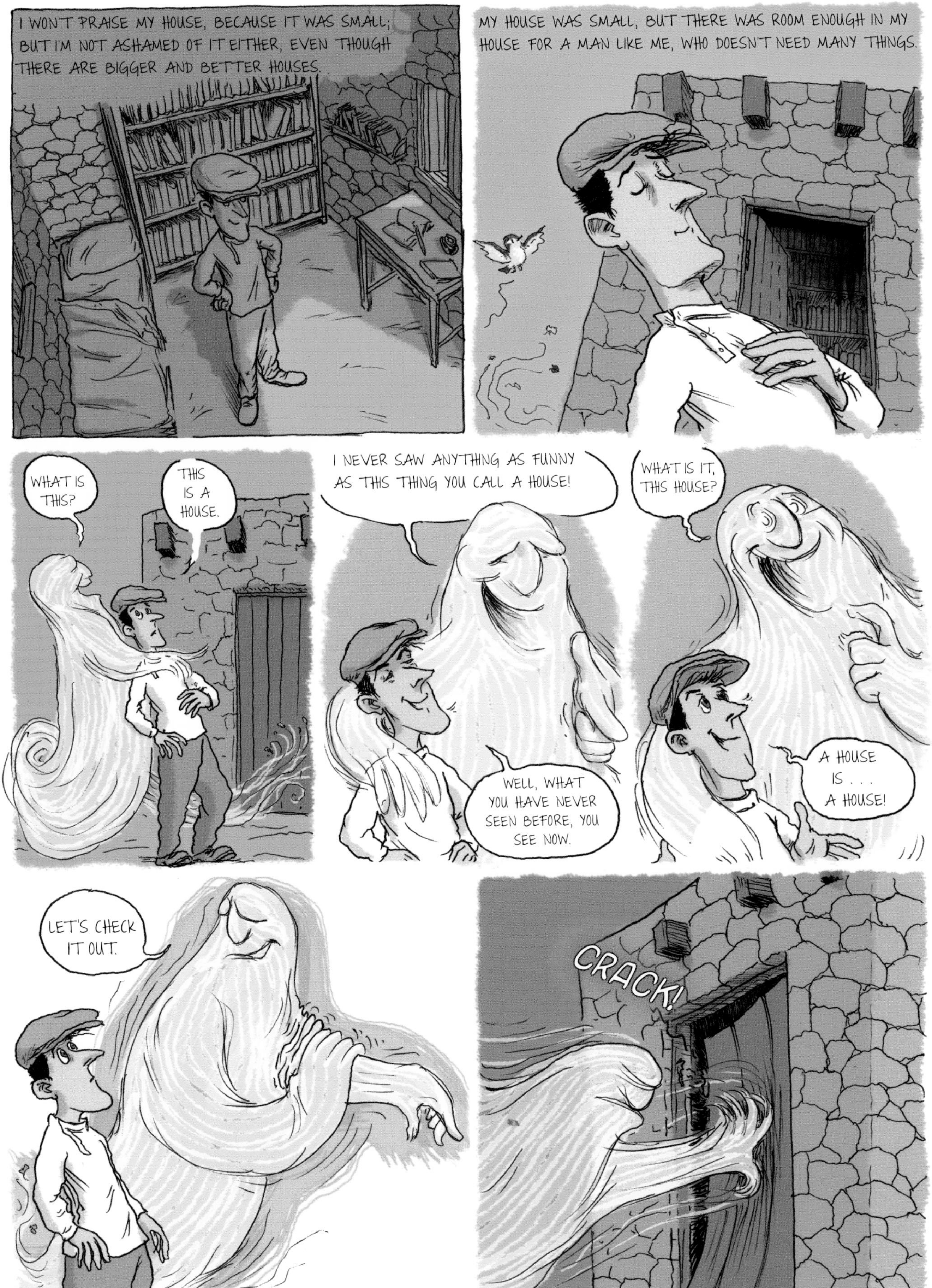
I WON'T PRAISE MY HOUSE, BECAUSE IT WAS SMALL; BUT I'M NOT ASHAMED OF IT EITHER, EVEN THOUGH THERE ARE BIGGER AND BETTER HOUSES.
MY HOUSE WAS SMALL, BUT THERE WAS ROOM ENOUGH IN MY HOUSE FOR A MAN LIKE ME, WHO DOESN'T NEED MANY THINGS.
WHAT IS THIS?
THIS IS A HOUSE.
I NEVER SAW ANYTHING AS FUNNY AS THIS THING YOU CALL A HOUSE!
WELL, WHAT YOU HAVE NEVER SEEN BEFORE, YOU SEE NOW.
WHAT IS IT, THIS HOUSE?
A HOUSE IS . . . A HOUSE!
LET'S CHECK IT OUT.
CRACK!

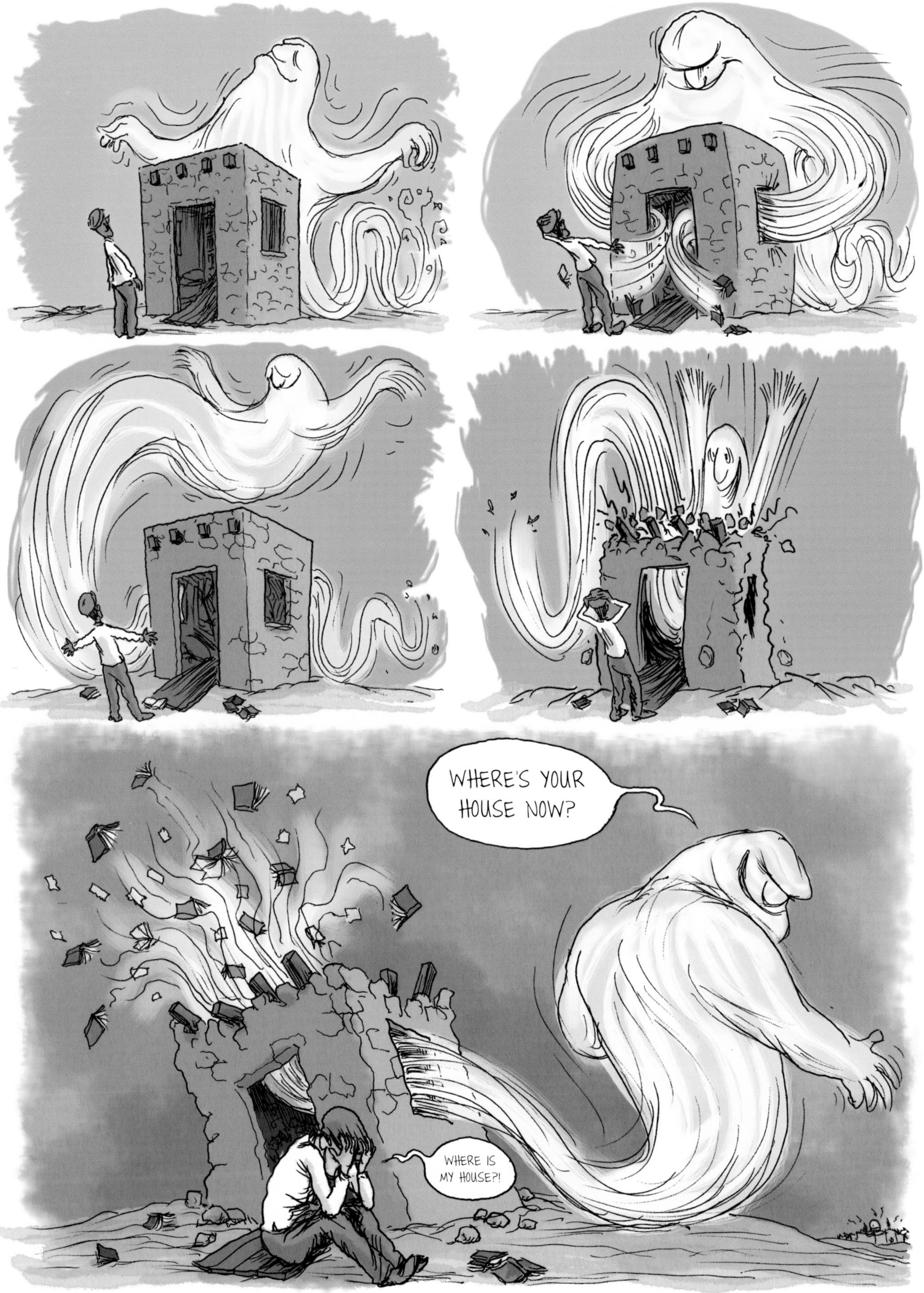
WHERE'S YOUR HOUSE NOW?
WHERE IS MY HOUSE?!

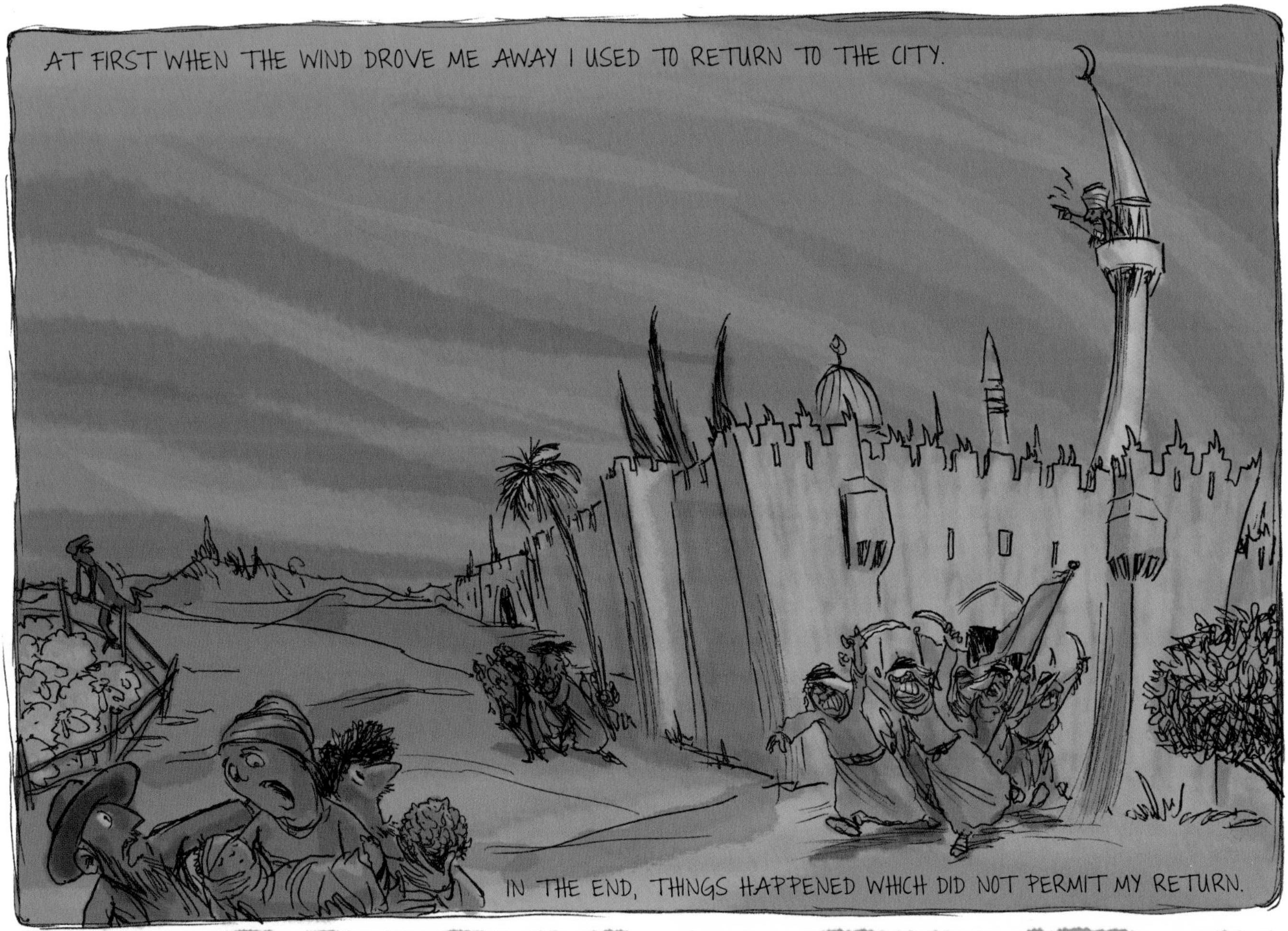
AT FIRST WHEN THE WIND DROVE ME AWAY I USED TO RETURN TO THE CITY.
IN THE END, THINGS HAPPENED WHICH DID NOT PERMIT MY RETURN.

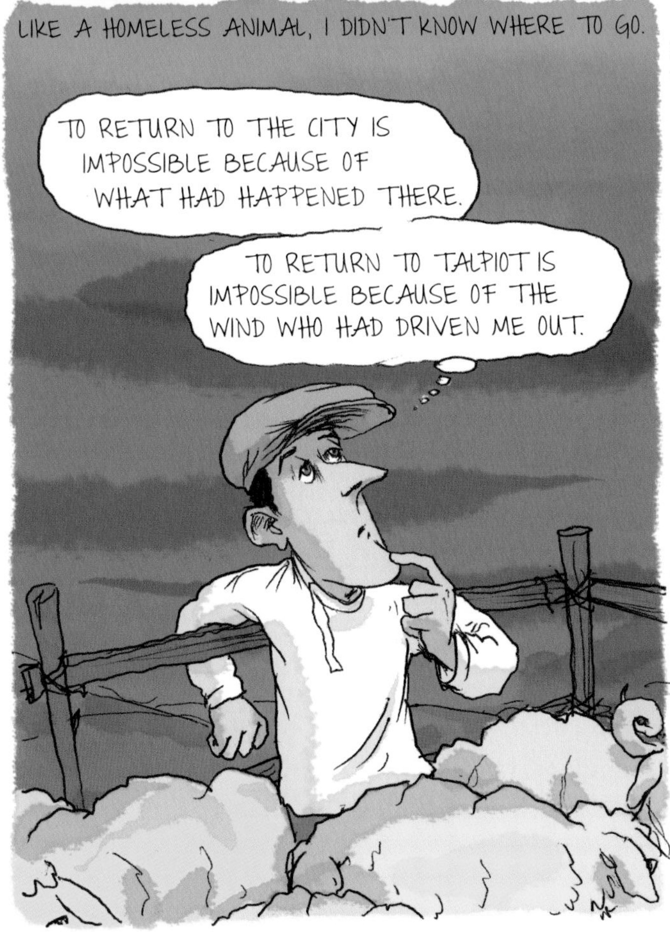
LIKE A HOMELESS ANIMAL, I DIDN'T KNOW WHERE TO GO.
TO RETURN TO THE CITY IS IMPOSSIBLE BECAUSE OF WHAT HAD HAPPENED THERE.
TO RETURN TO TALPIOT IS IMPOSSIBLE BECAUSE OF THE WIND WHO HAD DRIVEN ME OUT.

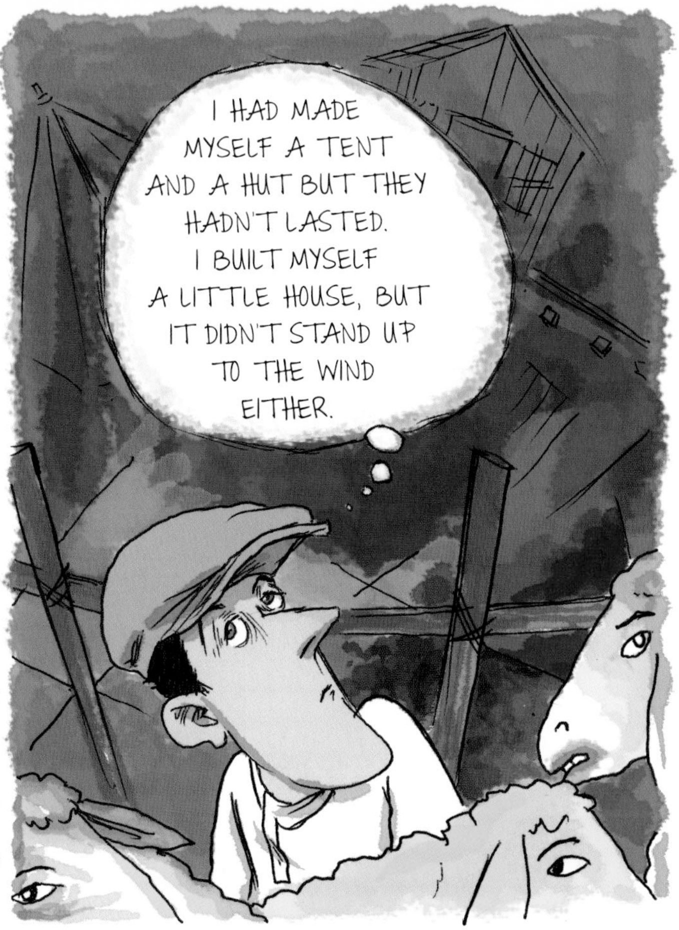
I HAD MADE MYSELF A TENT AND A HUT BUT THEY HADN'T LASTED. I BUILT MYSELF A LITTLE HOUSE, BUT IT DIDN'T STAND UP TO THE WIND EITHER.

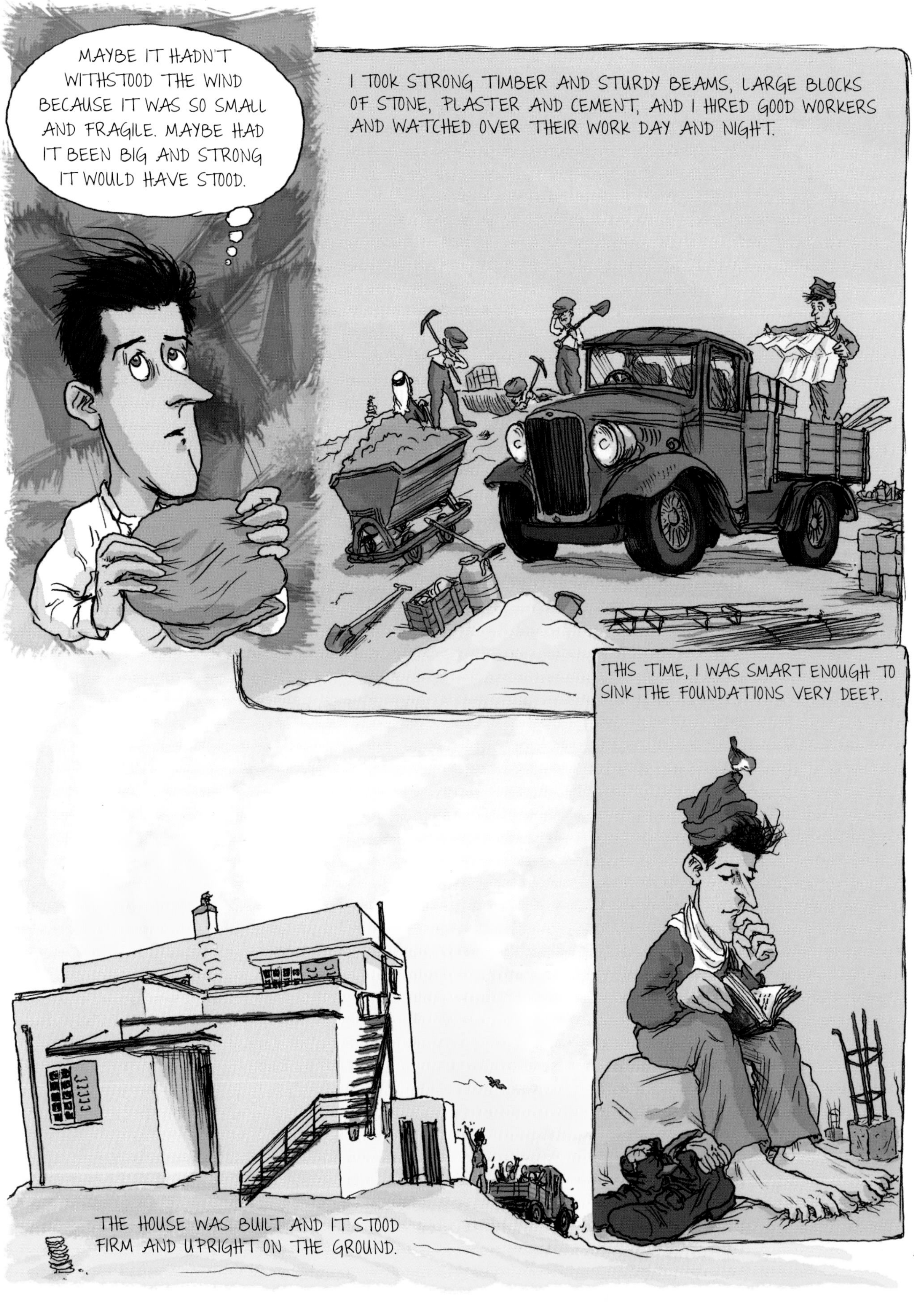
MAYBE IT HADN'T WITHSTOOD THE WIND BECAUSE IT WAS SO SMALL AND FRAGILE. MAYBE HAD IT BEEN BIG AND STRONG IT WOULD HAVE STOOD.
I TOOK STRONG TIMBER AND STURDY BEAMS, LARGE BLOCKS OF STONE, PLASTER AND CEMENT, AND I HIRED GOOD WORKERS AND WATCHED OVER THEIR WORK DAY AND NIGHT.
THIS TIME, I WAS SMART ENOUGH TO SINK THE FOUNDATIONS VERY DEEP.
THE HOUSE WAS BUILT AND IT STOOD FIRM AND UPRIGHT ON THE GROUND.

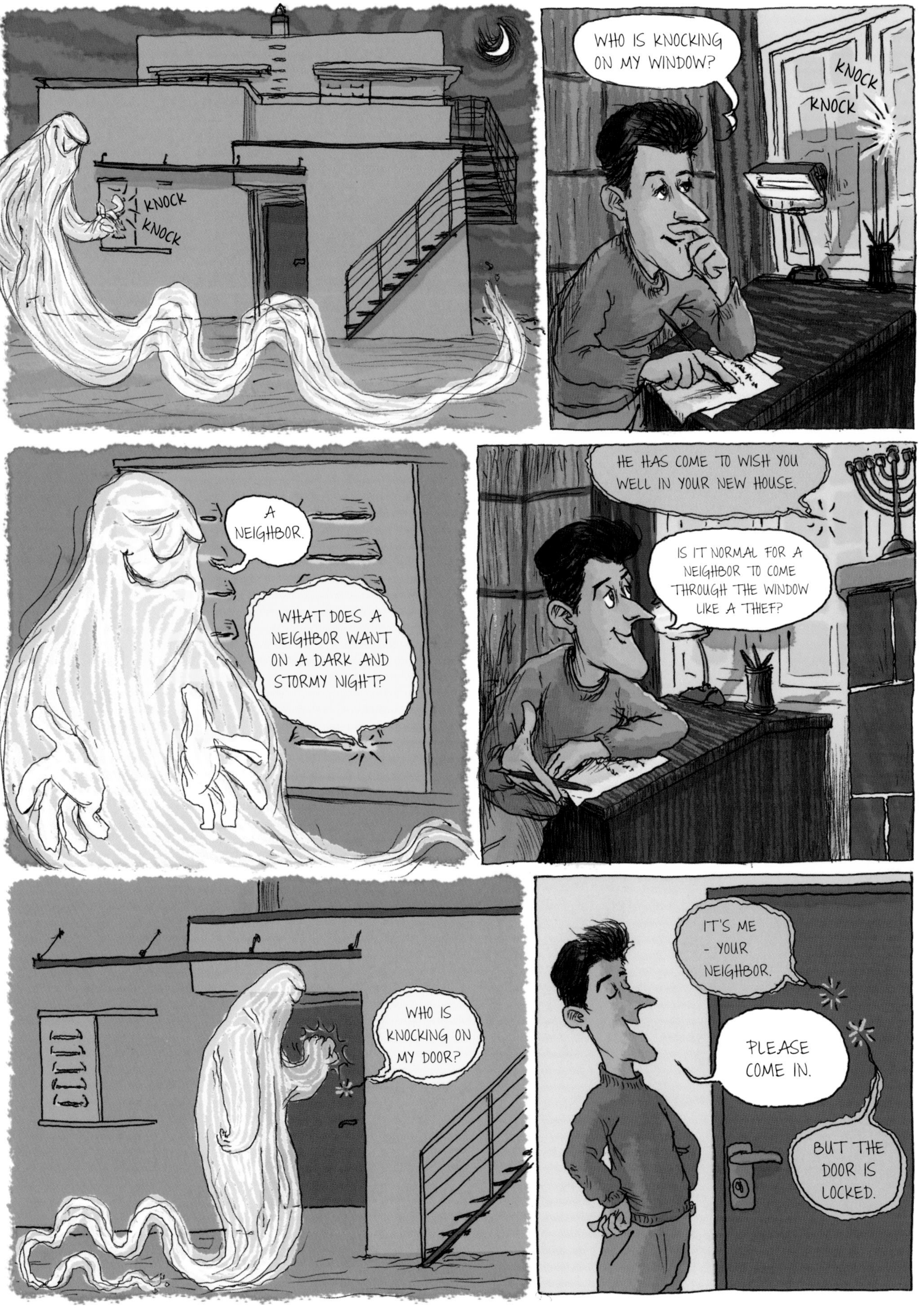
KNOCK
KNOCK
WHO IS KNOCKING ON MY WINDOW?
KNOCK
KNOCK
A NEIGHBOR.
WHAT DOES A NEIGHBOR WANT ON A DARK AND STORMY NIGHT?
HE HAS COME TO WISH YOU WELL IN YOUR NEW HOUSE.
IS IT NORMAL FOR A NEIGHBOR TO COME THROUGH THE WINDOW LIKE A THIEF?
WHO IS KNOCKING ON MY DOOR?
IT'S ME - YOUR NEIGHBOR.
PLEASE COME IN.
BUT THE DOOR IS LOCKED.

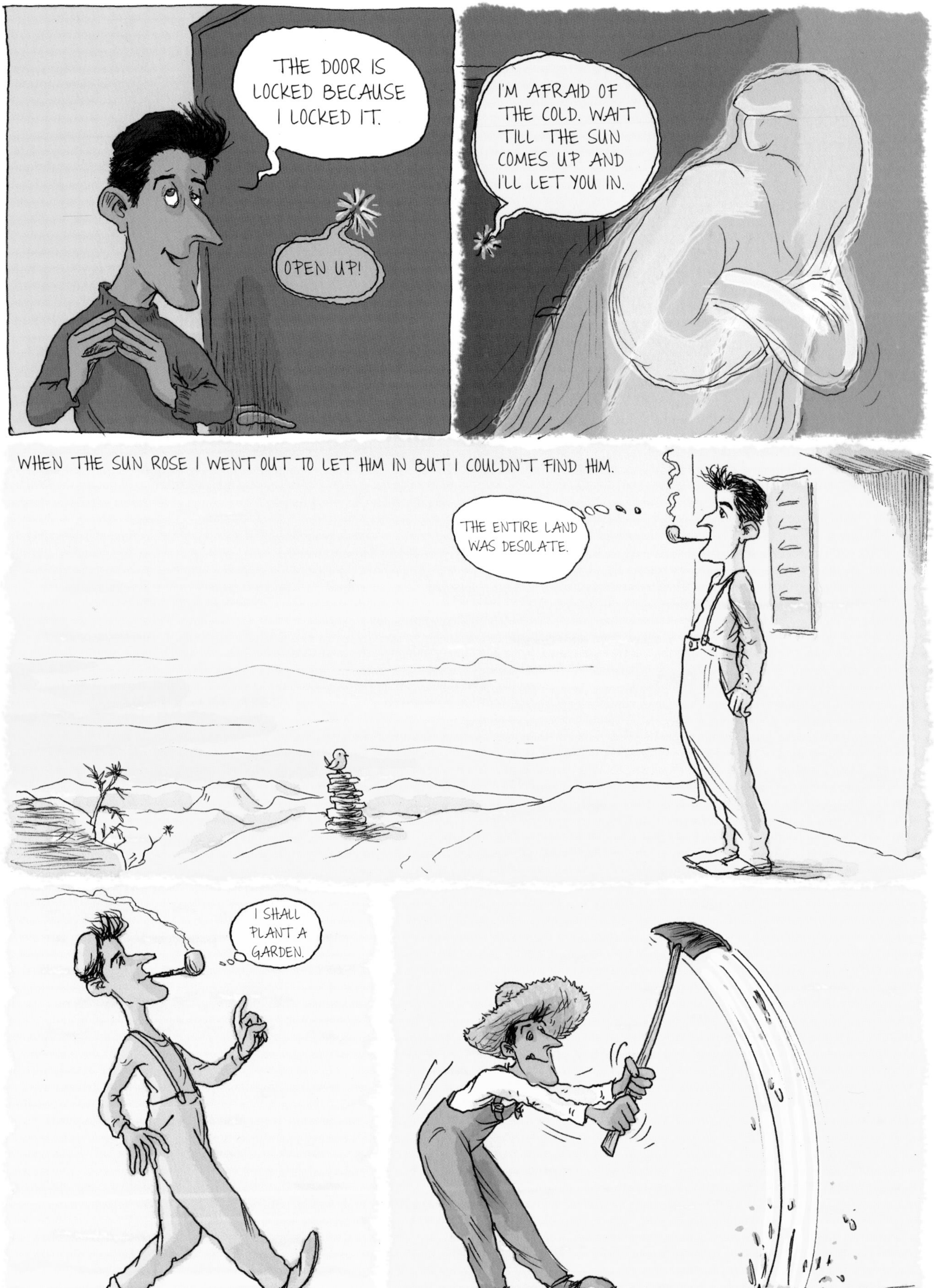
THE DOOR IS LOCKED BECAUSE I LOCKED IT.
OPEN UP!
I'M AFRAID OF THE COLD. WAIT TILL THE SUN COMES UP AND I'LL LET YOU IN.
WHEN THE SUN ROSE I WENT OUT TO LET HIM IN BUT I COULDN'T FIND HIM.
THE ENTIRE LAND WAS DESOLATE.
I SHALL PLANT A GARDEN.

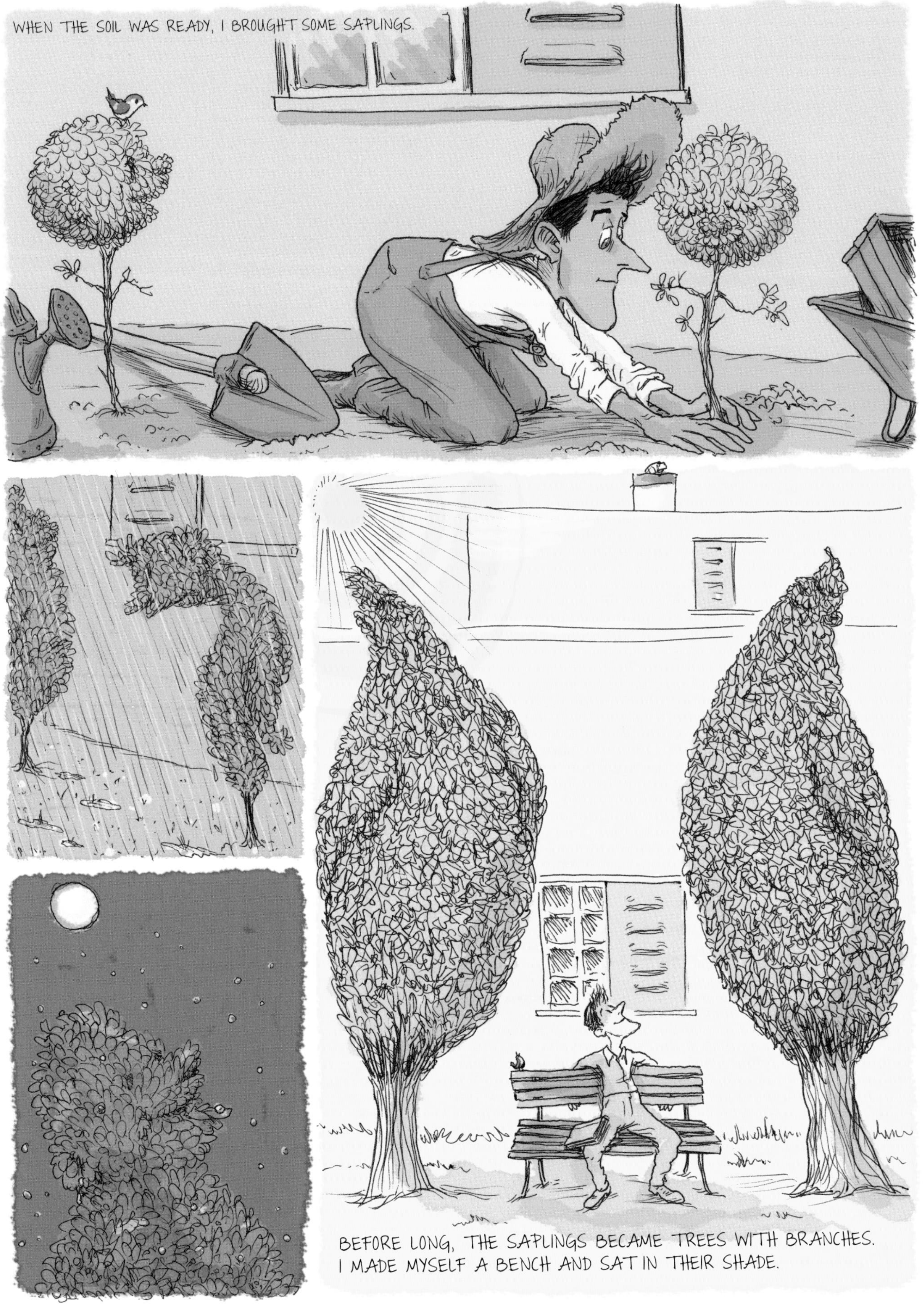
WHEN THE SOIL WAS READY, I BROUGHT SOME SAPLINGS.
BEFORE LONG, THE SAPLINGS BECAME TREES WITH BRANCHES.
I MADE MYSELF A BENCH AND SAT IN THEIR SHADE.

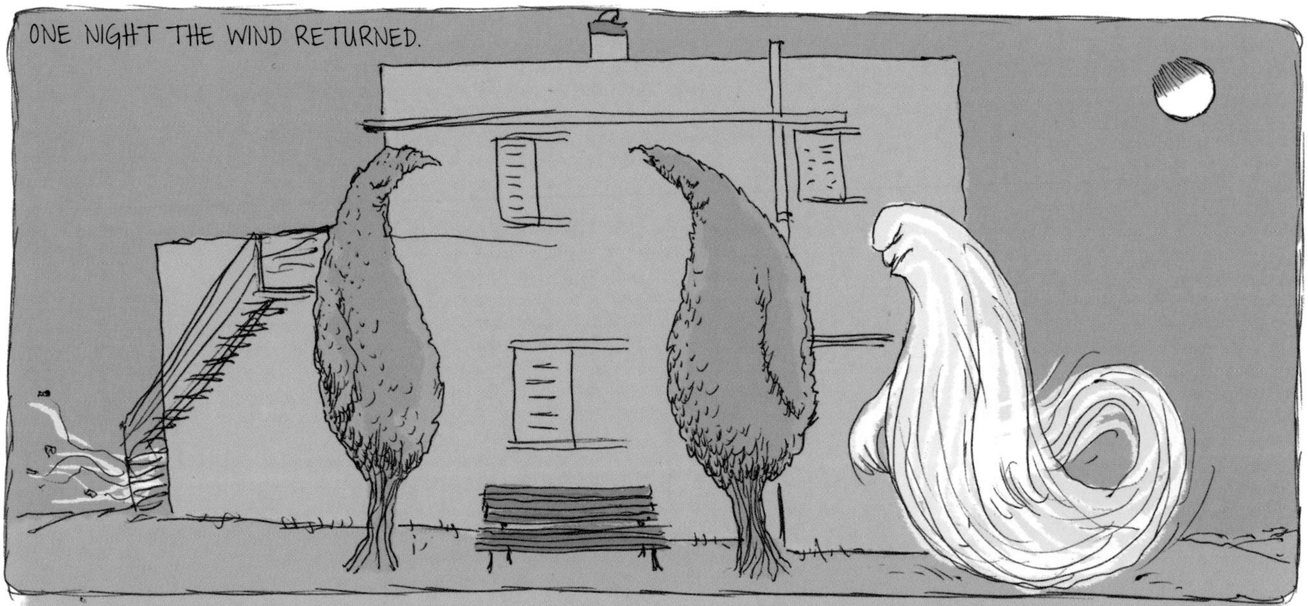
ONE NIGHT THE WIND RETURNED.

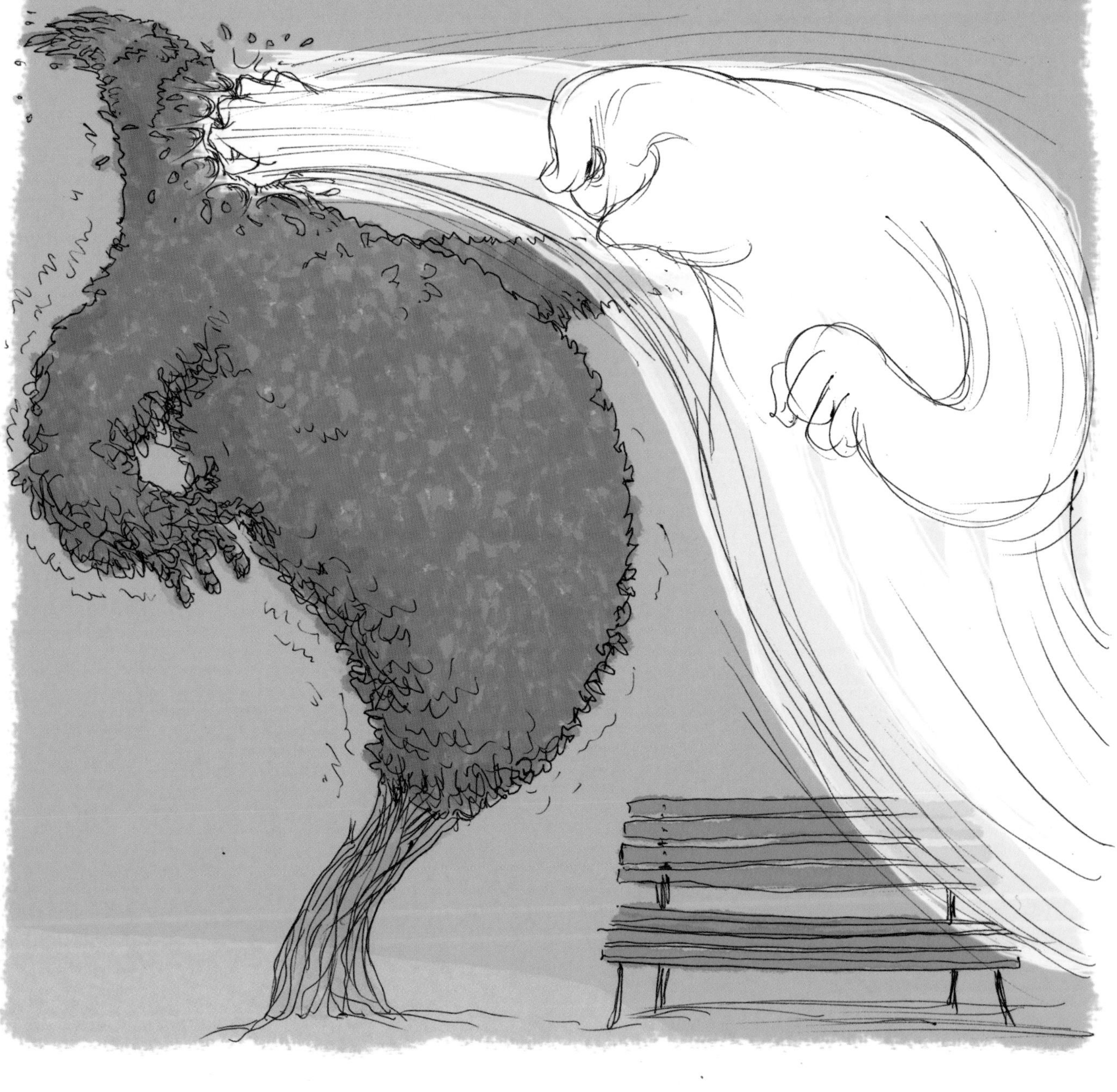

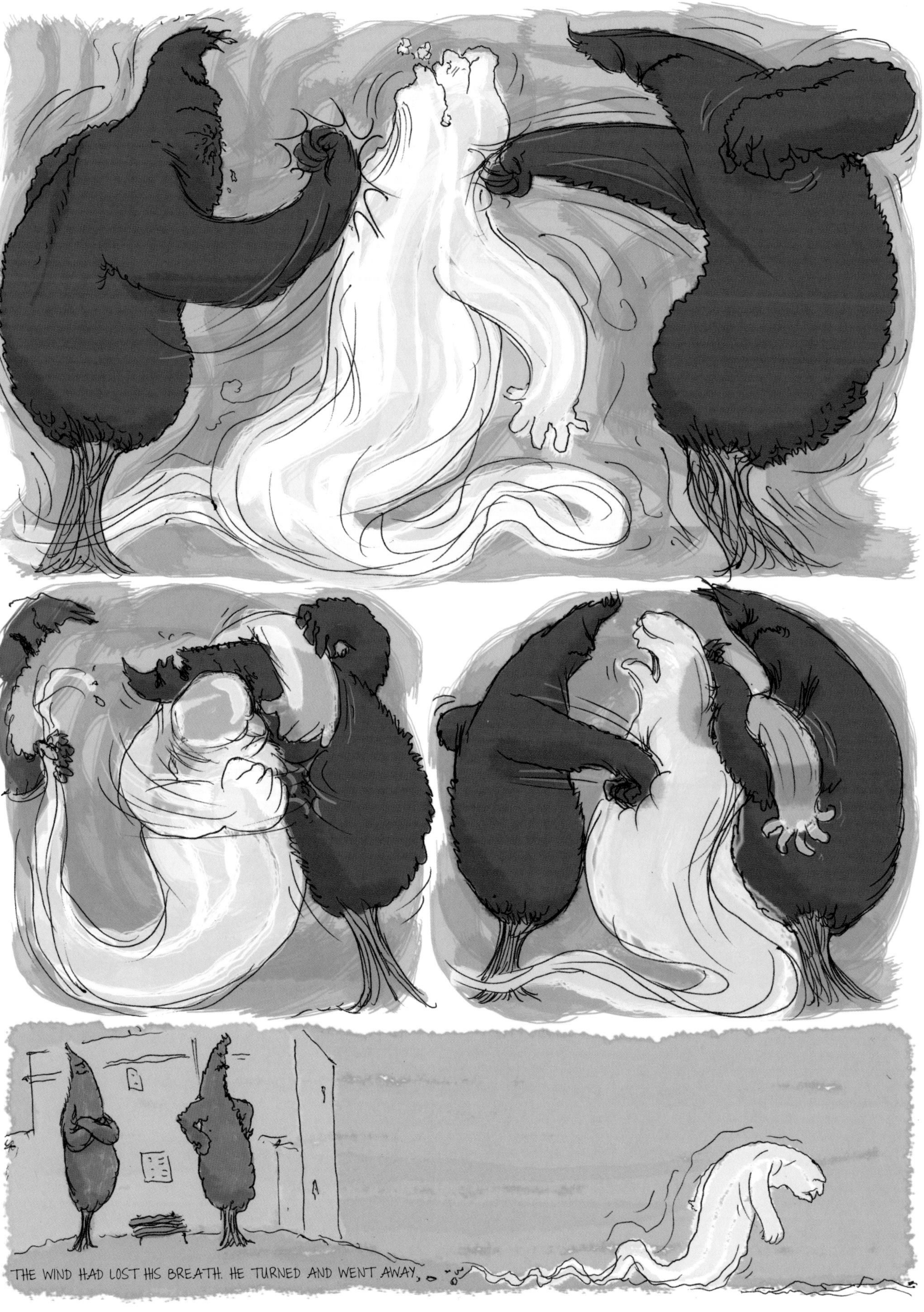
THE WIND HAD LOST HIS BREATH. HE TURNED AND WENT AWAY.

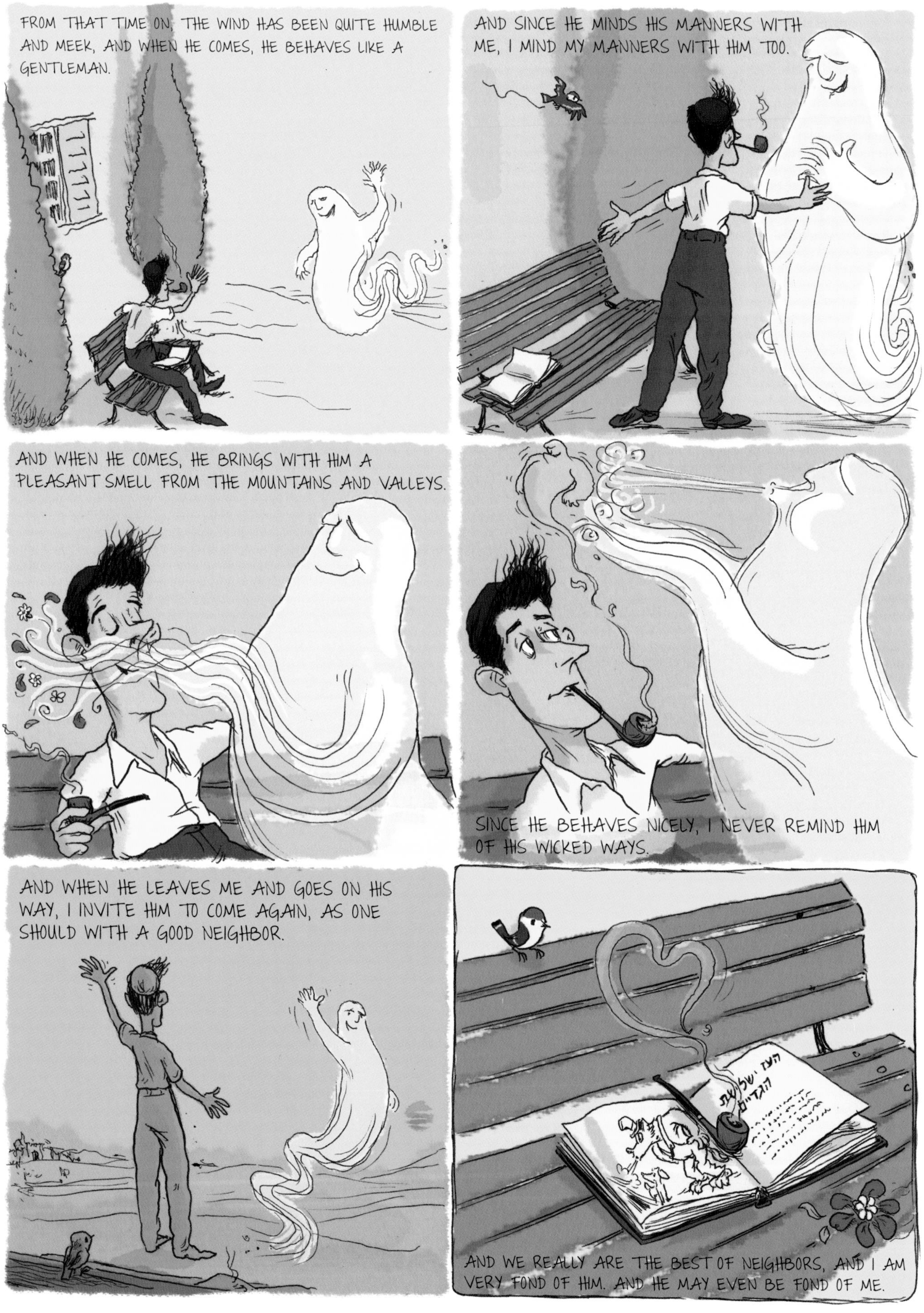
FROM THAT TIME ON, THE WIND HAS BEEN QUITE HUMBLE AND MEEK, AND WHEN HE COMES, HE BEHAVES LIKE A GENTLEMAN.
AND SINCE HE MINDS HIS MANNERS WITH ME, I MIND MY MANNERS WITH HIM TOO.
AND WHEN HE COMES, HE BRINGS WITH HIM A PLEASANT SMELL FROM THE MOUNTAINS AND VALLEYS.
SINCE HE BEHAVES NICELY, I NEVER REMIND HIM OF HIS WICKED WAYS.
AND WHEN HE LEAVES ME AND GOES ON HIS WAY, I INVITE HIM TO COME AGAIN, AS ONE SHOULD WITH A GOOD NEIGHBOR.
AND WE REALLY ARE THE BEST OF NEIGHBORS, AND I AM VERY FOND OF HIM. AND HE MAY EVEN BE FOND OF ME.

THE FABLE OF THE GOAT

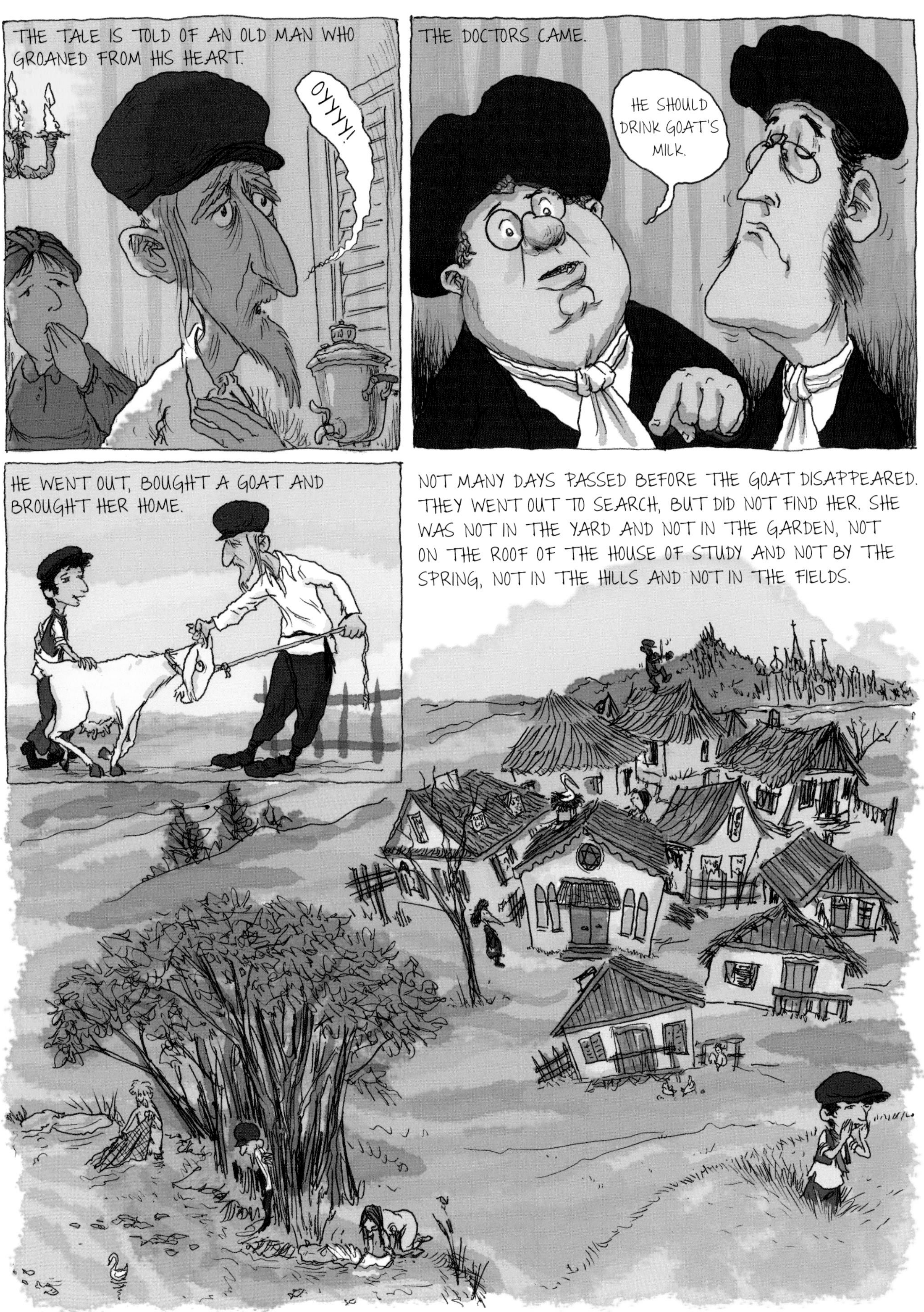
THE TALE IS TOLD OF AN OLD MAN WHO GROANED FROM HIS HEART.
OYYYY!
THE DOCTORS CAME.
HE SHOULD DRINK GOAT'S MILK.
HE WENT OUT, BOUGHT A GOAT AND BROUGHT HER HOME.
NOT MANY DAYS PASSED BEFORE THE GOAT DISAPPEARED. THEY WENT OUT TO SEARCH, BUT DID NOT FIND HER. SHE WAS NOT IN THE YARD AND NOT IN THE GARDEN, NOT ON THE ROOF OF THE HOUSE OF STUDY AND NOT BY THE SPRING, NOT IN THE HILLS AND NOT IN THE FIELDS.

SHE WAITED SEVERAL DAYS AND THEN RETURNED BY HERSELF.

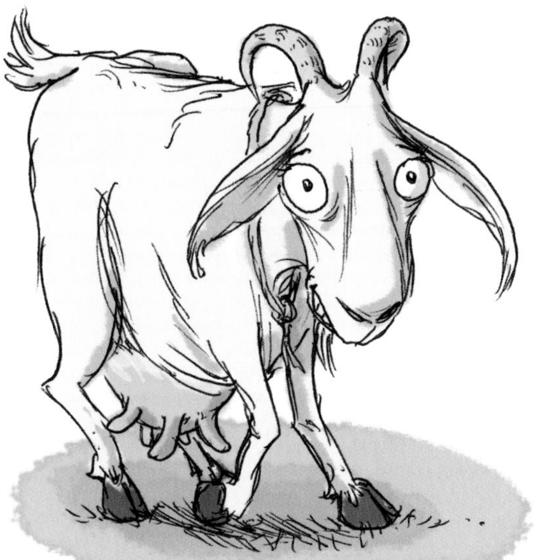

WHEN SHE RETURNED, HER UDDER WAS FULL OF MILK,

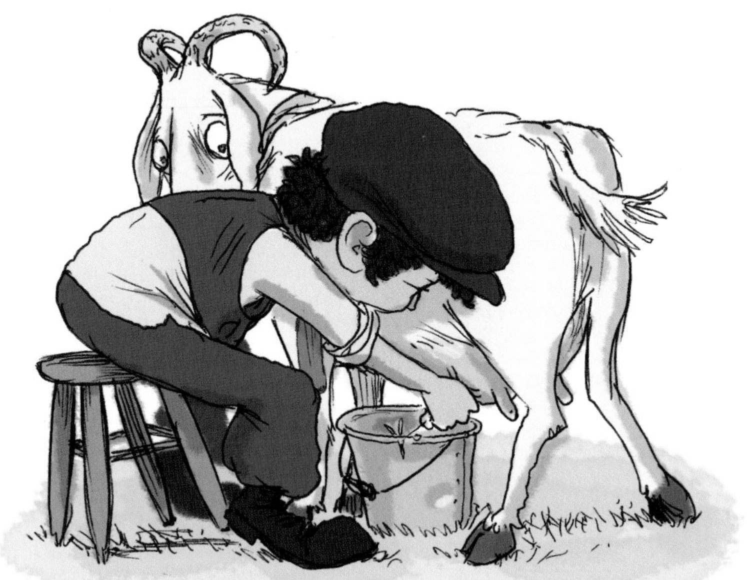

THE TASTE OF WHICH WAS THE TASTE OF THE GARDEN OF EDEN.

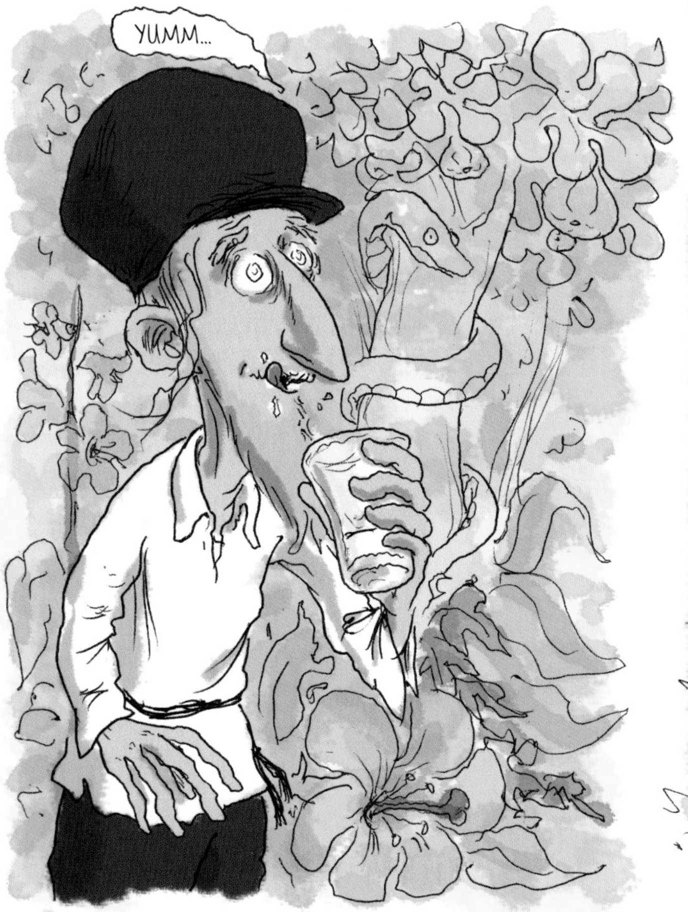
YUMM...

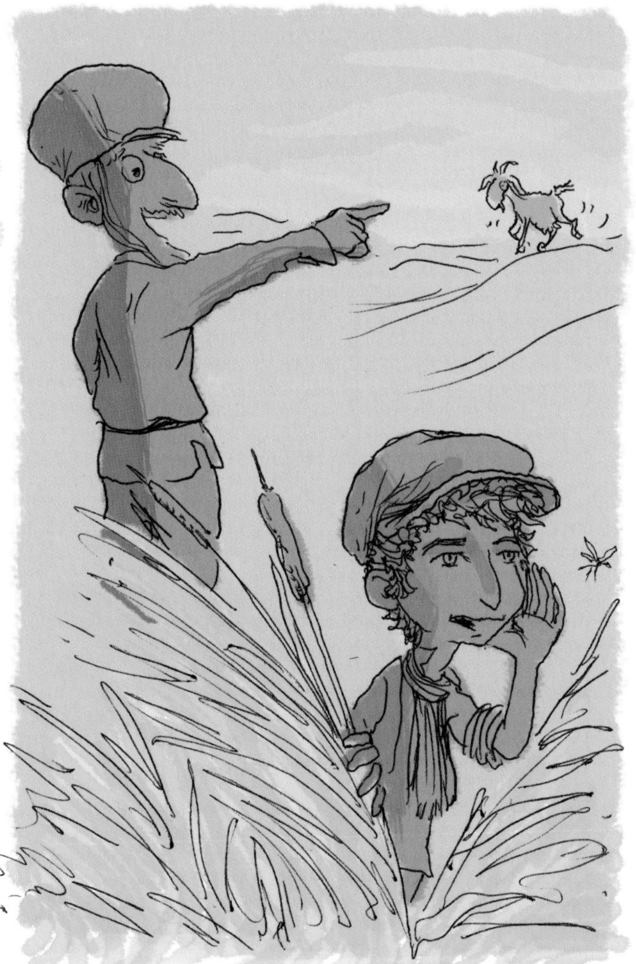

NOT JUST ONCE, BUT MANY TIMES SHE DISAPPEARED FROM THE HOUSE. THEY WOULD GO OUT IN SEARCH OF HER AND WOULD NOT FIND HER UNTIL SHE RETURNED BY HERSELF WITH HER UDDER FULL OF MILK THAT WAS SWEETER THAN HONEY AND WHOSE TASTE WAS THE TASTE OF THE GARDEN OF EDEN.

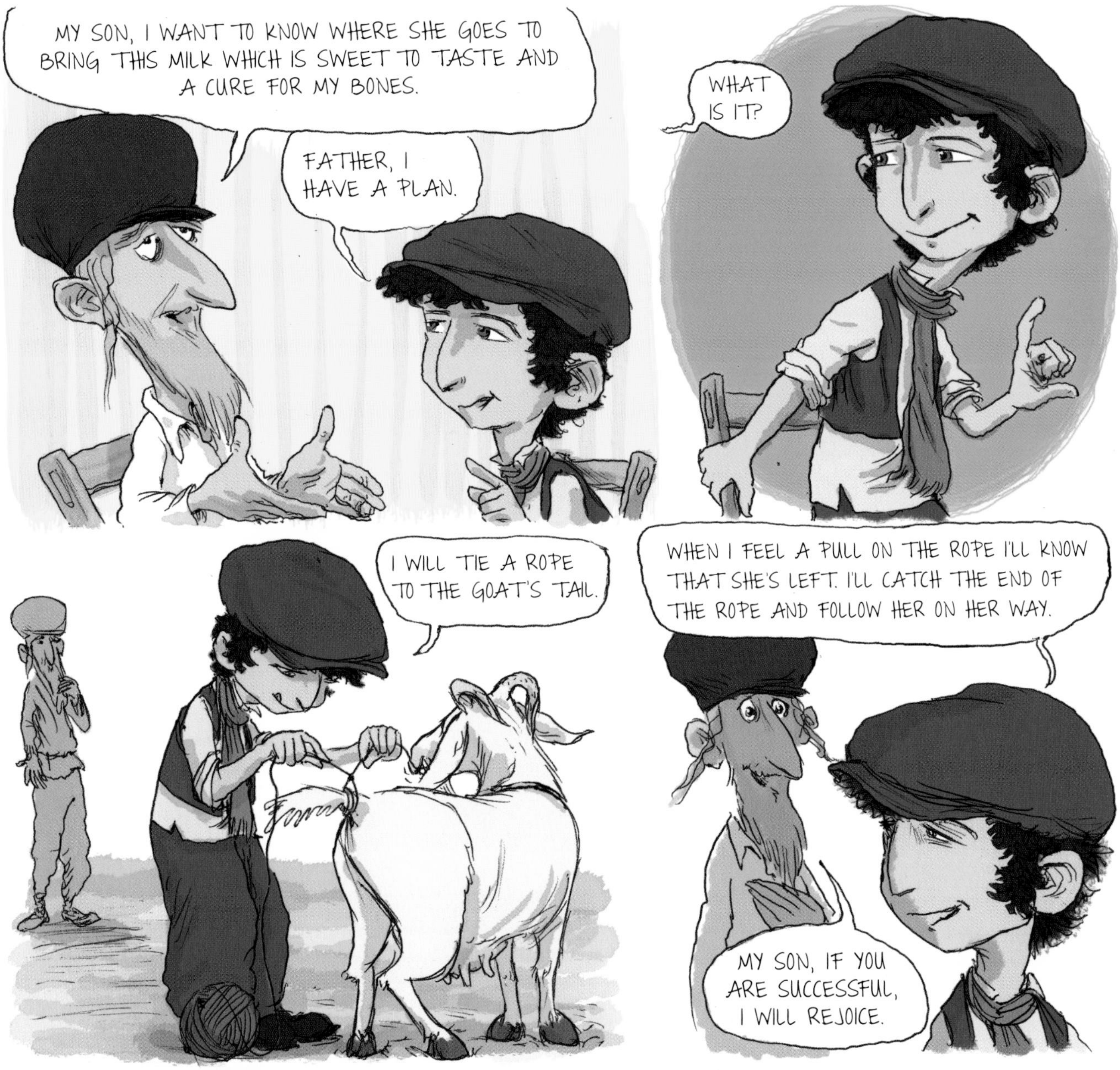
MY SON, I WANT TO KNOW WHERE SHE GOES TO BRING THIS MILK WHICH IS SWEET TO TASTE AND A CURE FOR MY BONES.
FATHER, I HAVE A PLAN.
WHAT IS IT?
I WILL TIE A ROPE TO THE GOAT'S TAIL.
WHEN I FEEL A PULL ON THE ROPE I'LL KNOW THAT SHE'S LEFT. I'LL CATCH THE END OF THE ROPE AND FOLLOW HER ON HER WAY.
MY SON, IF YOU ARE SUCCESSFUL, I WILL REJOICE.

THE BOY TIED THE ROPE TO THE GOAT'S TAIL AND WATCHED IT CAREFULLY. WHEN THE GOAT SET OFF, HE HELD THE ROPE IN HIS HAND AND DID NOT LET GO UNTIL THE GOAT WAS ON HER WAY AND HE WAS FOLLOWING HER.

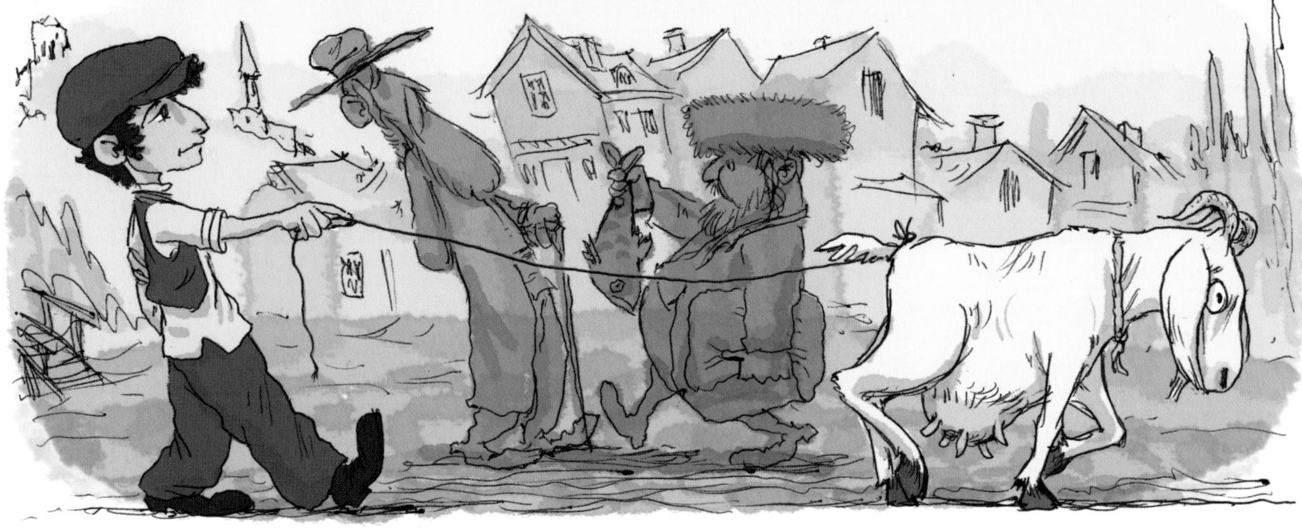

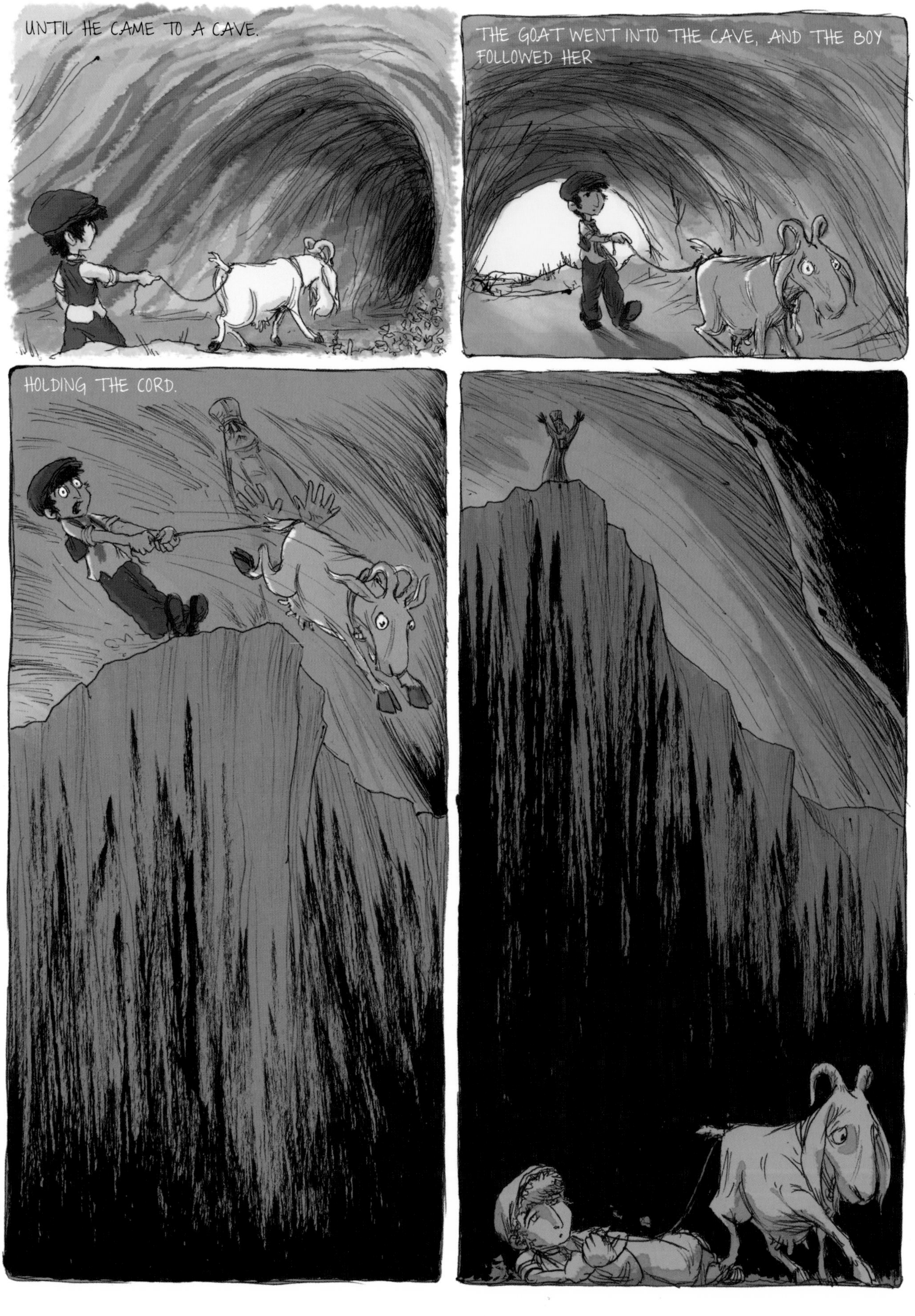
UNTIL HE CAME TO A CAVE.
THE GOAT WENT INTO THE CAVE, AND THE BOY FOLLOWED HER
HOLDING THE CORD.

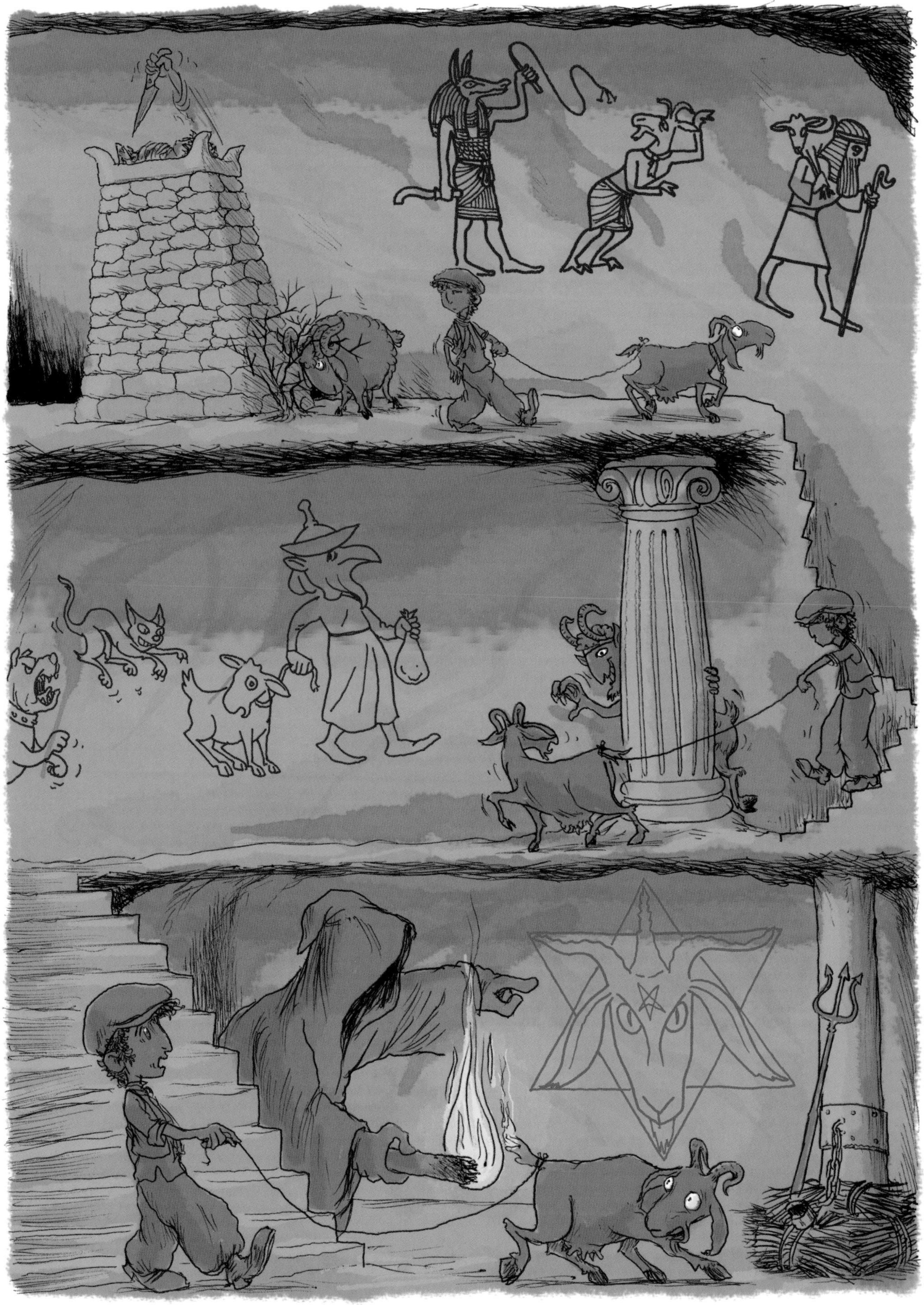

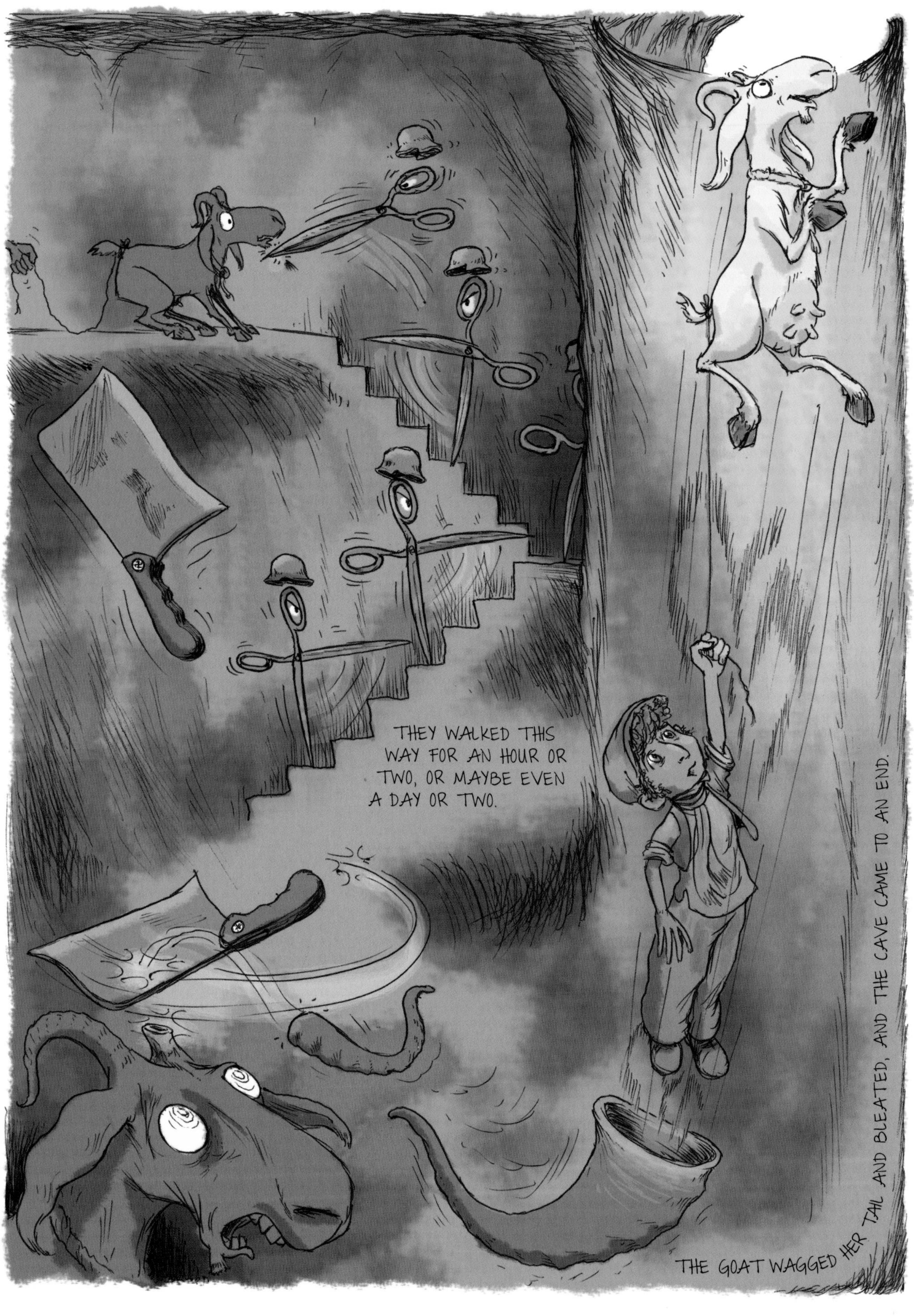
THEY WALKED THIS WAY FOR AN HOUR OR TWO, OR MAYBE EVEN A DAY OR TWO.
THE GOAT WAGGED HER TAIL AND BLEATED, AND THE CAVE CAME TO AN END.

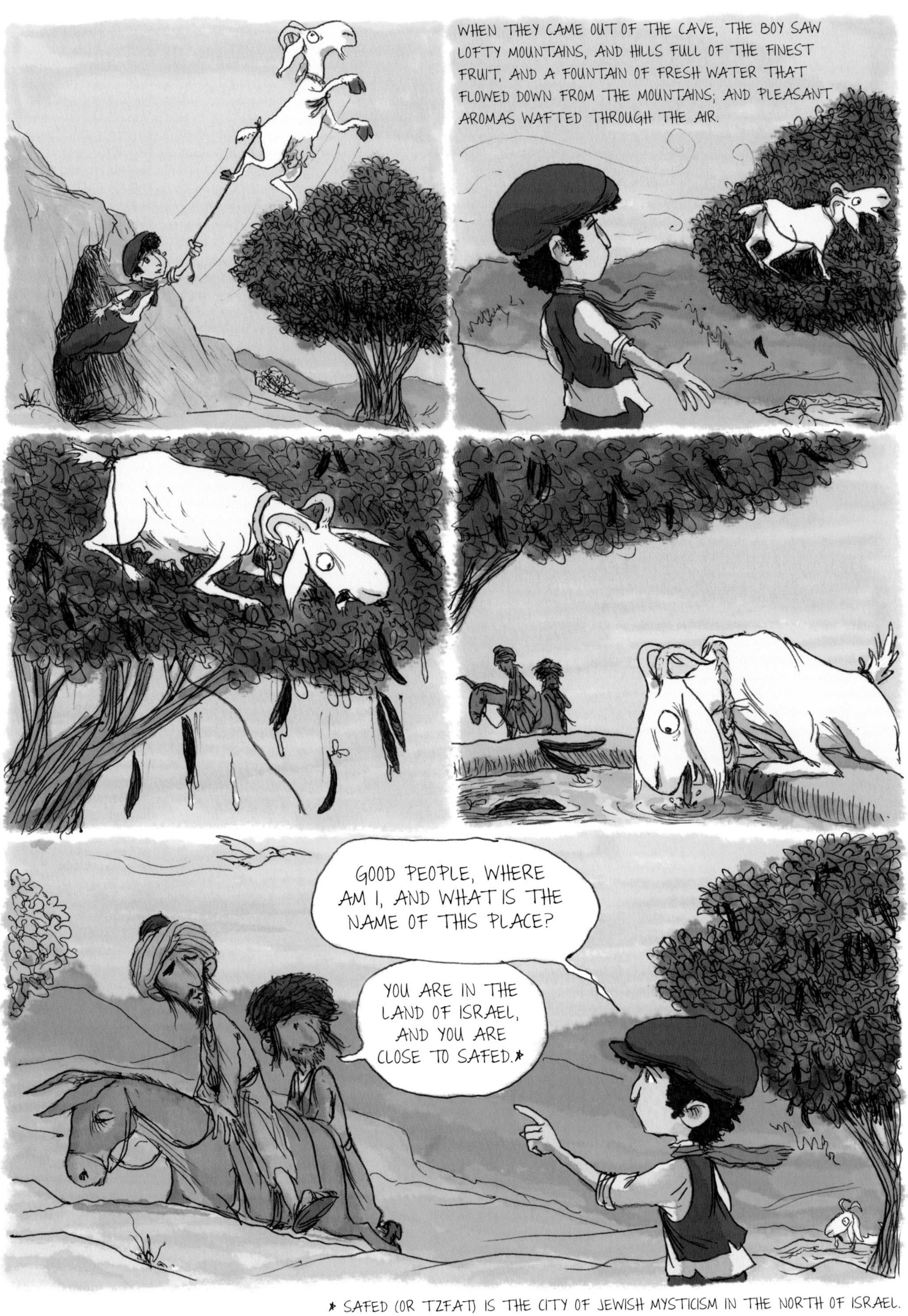
WHEN THEY CAME OUT OF THE CAVE, THE BOY SAW LOFTY MOUNTAINS, AND HILLS FULL OF THE FINEST FRUIT, AND A FOUNTAIN OF FRESH WATER THAT FLOWED DOWN FROM THE MOUNTAINS; AND PLEASANT AROMAS WAFTED THROUGH THE AIR.
GOOD PEOPLE, WHERE AM I, AND WHAT IS THE NAME OF THIS PLACE?
YOU ARE IN THE LAND OF ISRAEL, AND YOU ARE CLOSE TO SAFED.*

* SAFED (OR TZFAT) IS THE CITY OF JEWISH MYSTICISM IN THE NORTH OF ISRAEL.

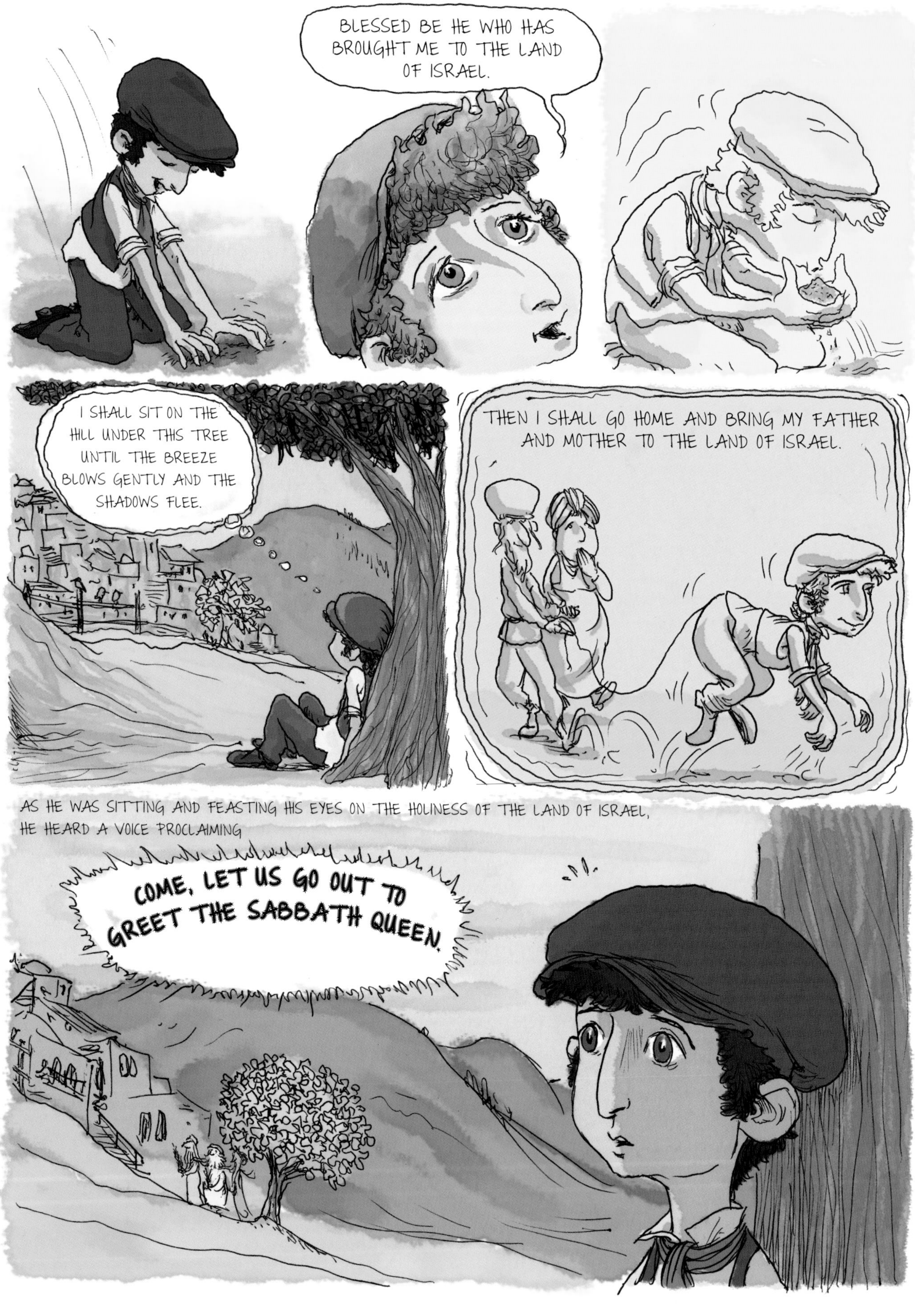

BLESSED BE HE WHO HAS BROUGHT ME TO THE LAND OF ISRAEL.
I SHALL SIT ON THE HILL UNDER THIS TREE UNTIL THE BREEZE BLOWS GENTLY AND THE SHADOWS FLEE.
THEN I SHALL GO HOME AND BRING MY FATHER AND MOTHER TO THE LAND OF ISRAEL.
AS HE WAS SITTING AND FEASTING HIS EYES ON THE HOLINESS OF THE LAND OF ISRAEL, HE HEARD A VOICE PROCLAIMING
COME, LET US GO OUT TO GREET THE SABBATH QUEEN.

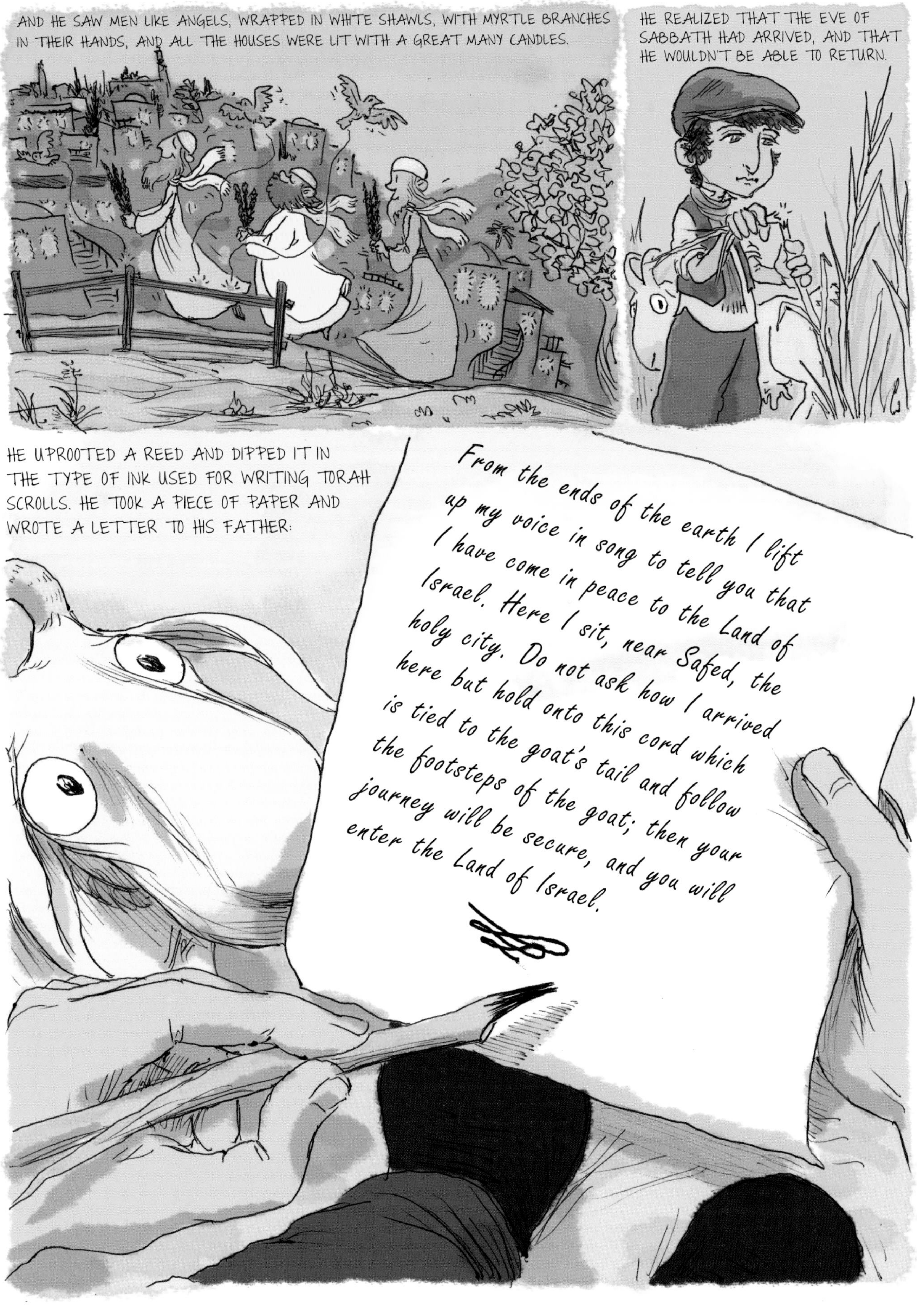
AND HE SAW MEN LIKE ANGELS, WRAPPED IN WHITE SHAWLS, WITH MYRTLE BRANCHES IN THEIR HANDS, AND ALL THE HOUSES WERE LIT WITH A GREAT MANY CANDLES.
HE REALIZED THAT THE EVE OF SABBATH HAD ARRIVED, AND THAT HE WOULDN'T BE ABLE TO RETURN.
HE UPROOTED A REED AND DIPPED IT IN THE TYPE OF INK USED FOR WRITING TORAH SCROLLS. HE TOOK A PIECE OF PAPER AND WROTE A LETTER TO HIS FATHER:
From the ends of the earth I lift up my voice in song to tell you that I have come in peace to the Land of Israel. Here I sit, near Safed, the holy city. Do not ask how I arrived here but hold onto this cord which is tied to the goat's tail and follow the footsteps of the goat; then your journey will be secure, and you will enter the Land of Israel.

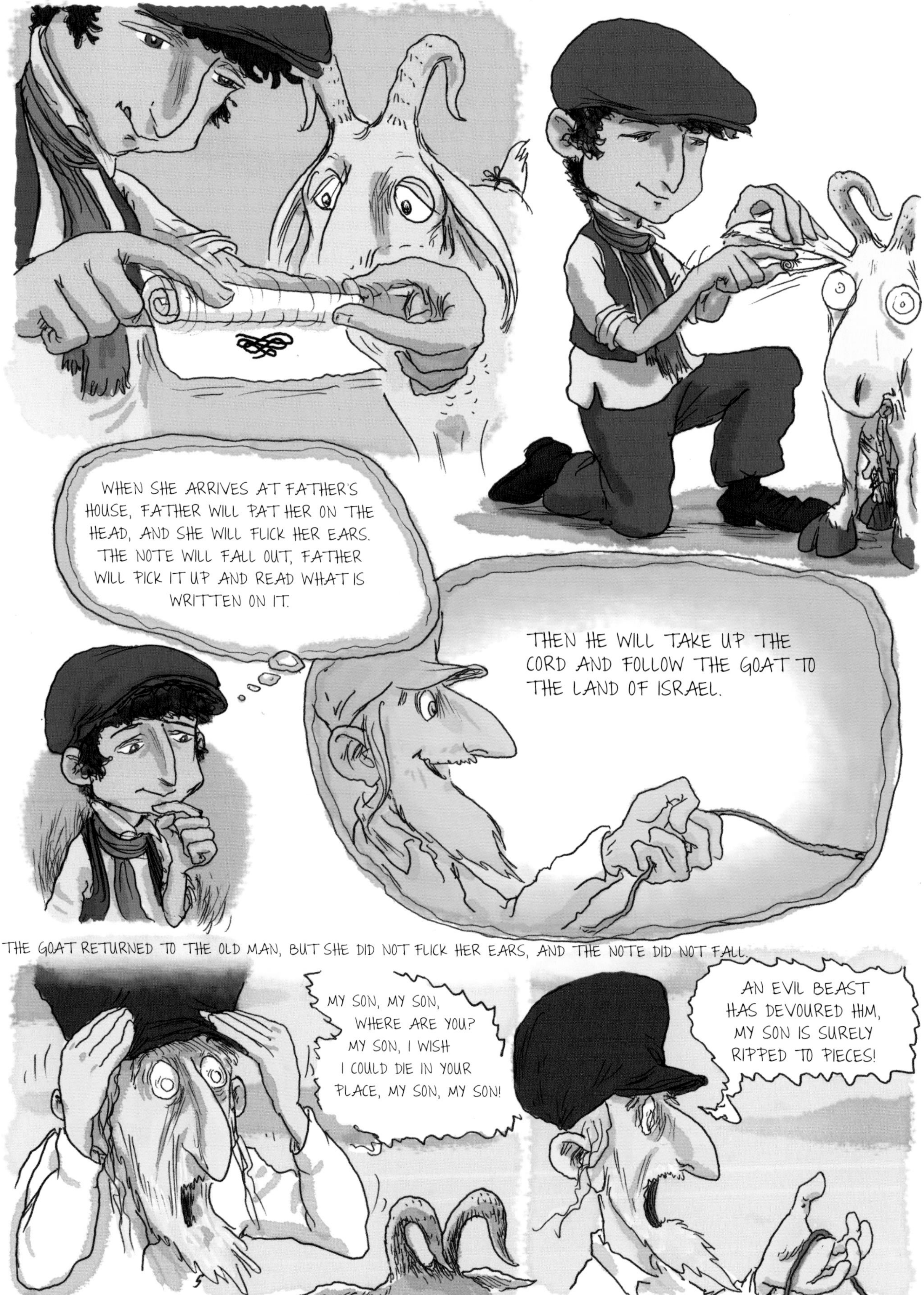
WHEN SHE ARRIVES AT FATHER'S HOUSE, FATHER WILL PAT HER ON THE HEAD, AND SHE WILL FLICK HER EARS. THE NOTE WILL FALL OUT, FATHER WILL PICK IT UP AND READ WHAT IS WRITTEN ON IT.
THEN HE WILL TAKE UP THE CORD AND FOLLOW THE GOAT TO THE LAND OF ISRAEL.
THE GOAT RETURNED TO THE OLD MAN, BUT SHE DID NOT FLICK HER EARS, AND THE NOTE DID NOT FALL.
MY SON, MY SON, WHERE ARE YOU? MY SON, I WISH I COULD DIE IN YOUR PLACE, MY SON, MY SON!
AN EVIL BEAST HAS DEVOURED HIM, MY SON IS SURELY RIPPED TO PIECES!

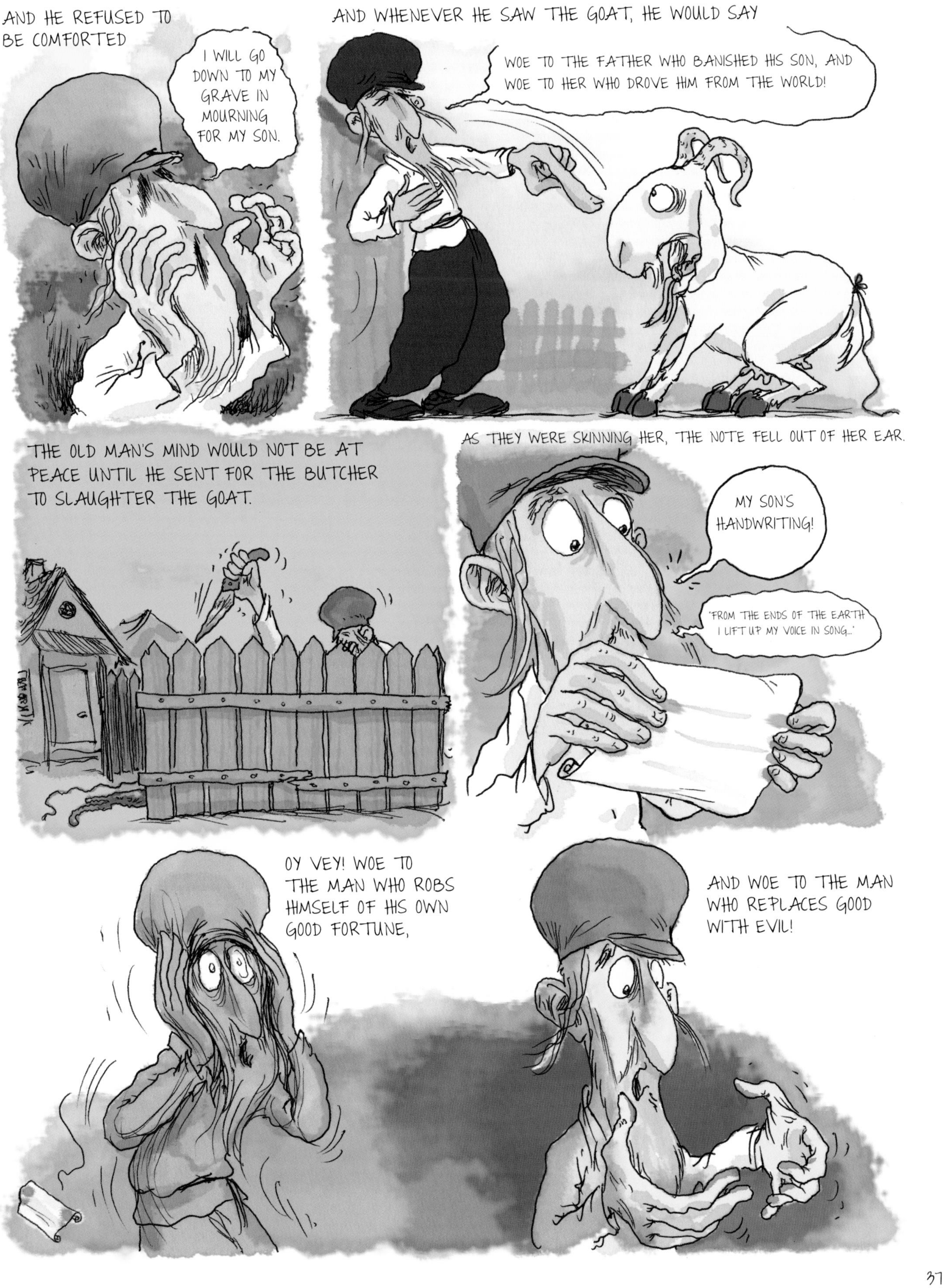
AND HE REFUSED TO BE COMFORTED
I WILL GO DOWN TO MY GRAVE IN MOURNING FOR MY SON.
AND WHENEVER HE SAW THE GOAT, HE WOULD SAY
WOE TO THE FATHER WHO BANISHED HIS SON, AND WOE TO HER WHO DROVE HIM FROM THE WORLD!
THE OLD MAN'S MIND WOULD NOT BE AT PEACE UNTIL HE SENT FOR THE BUTCHER TO SLAUGHTER THE GOAT.
AS THEY WERE SKINNING HER, THE NOTE FELL OUT OF HER EAR.
MY SON'S HANDWRITING!
"FROM THE ENDS OF THE EARTH I LIFT UP MY VOICE IN SONG..."
OY VEY! WOE TO THE MAN WHO ROBS HIMSELF OF HIS OWN GOOD FORTUNE,
AND WOE TO THE MAN WHO REPLACES GOOD WITH EVIL!

HE MOURNED OVER THE GOAT MANY DAYS AND REFUSED TO BE COMFORTED.

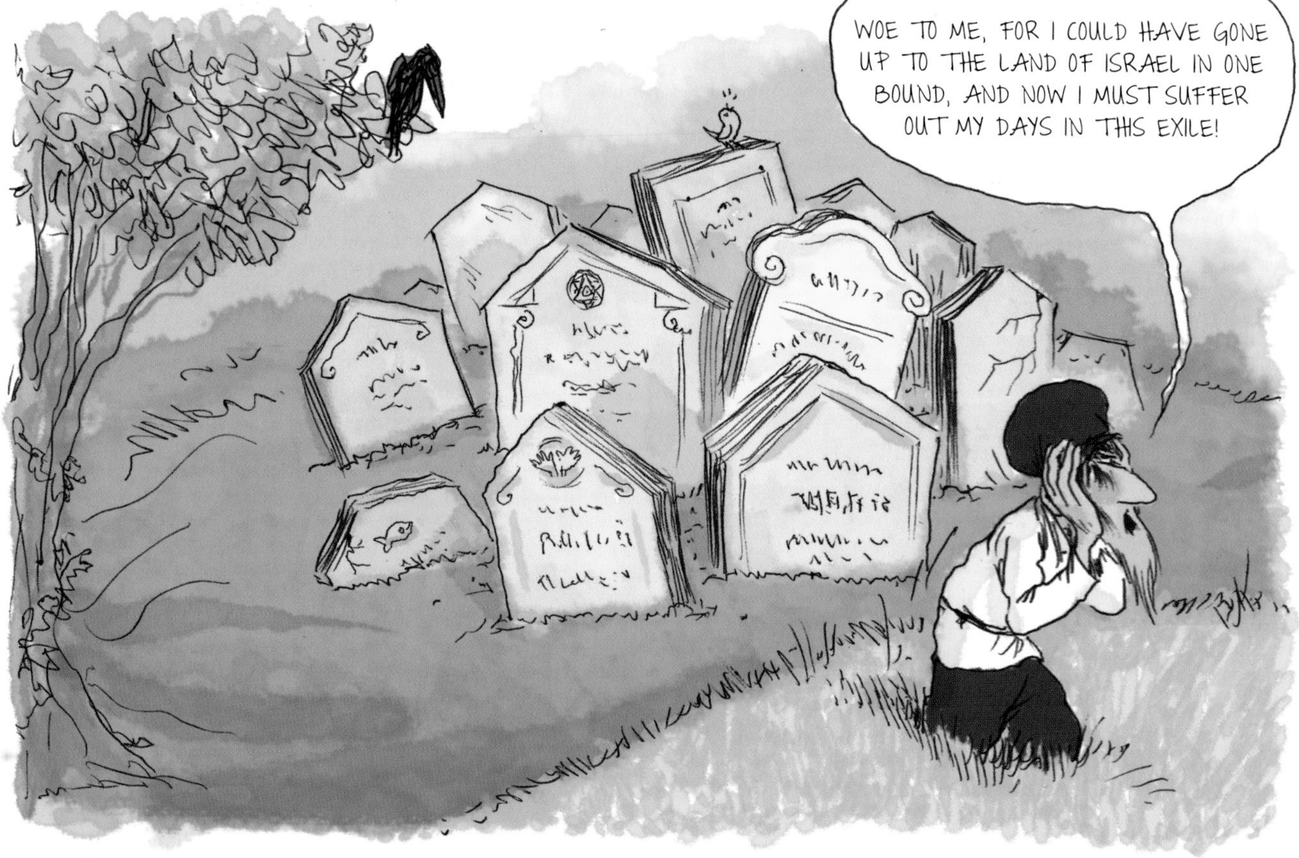
WOE TO ME, FOR I COULD HAVE GONE UP TO THE LAND OF ISRAEL IN ONE BOUND, AND NOW I MUST SUFFER OUT MY DAYS IN THIS EXILE!

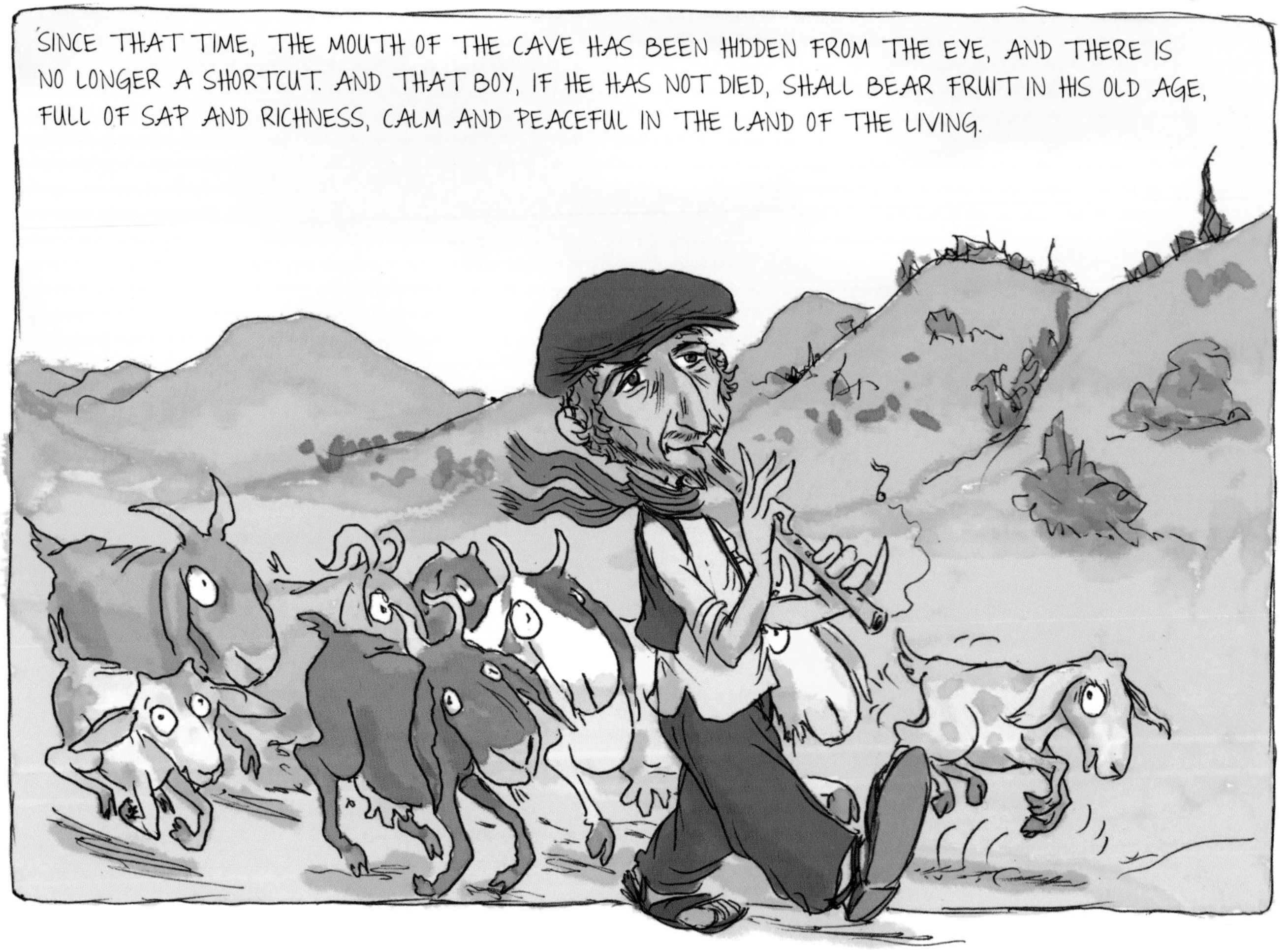
SINCE THAT TIME, THE MOUTH OF THE CAVE HAS BEEN HIDDEN FROM THE EYE, AND THERE IS NO LONGER A SHORTCUT. AND THAT BOY, IF HE HAS NOT DIED, SHALL BEAR FRUIT IN HIS OLD AGE, FULL OF SAP AND RICHNESS, CALM AND PEACEFUL IN THE LAND OF THE LIVING.

THE ARCHITECT AND THE EMPEROR

A TALE OF AN OLD ARCHITECT WHO WAS MUCH LOVED BY THE EMPEROR FOR DESIGNING PALACES, CASTLES, TEMPLES, AND FORTRESSES MORE BEAUTIFUL THAN ANY STRUCTURE BUILT BEFORE.

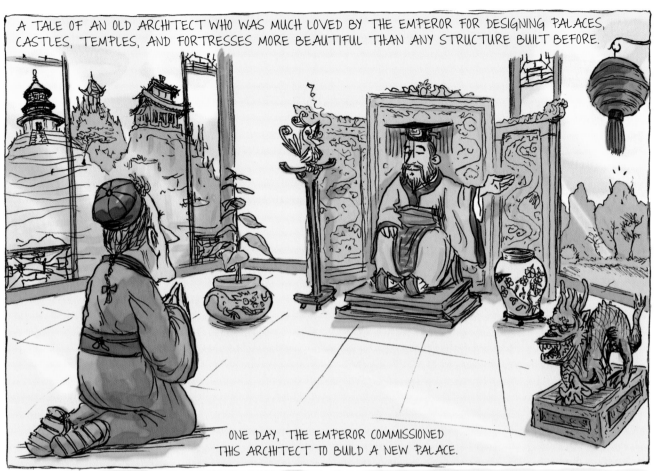

ONE DAY, THE EMPEROR COMMISSIONED THIS ARCHITECT TO BUILD A NEW PALACE.

YET YEARS WENT BY AND NOTHING WAS DONE, FOR THE ARCHITECT HAD LOST ALL INTEREST IN WORKING IN WOOD AND STONE.

THEY BEGAN TO PRESSURE HIM.

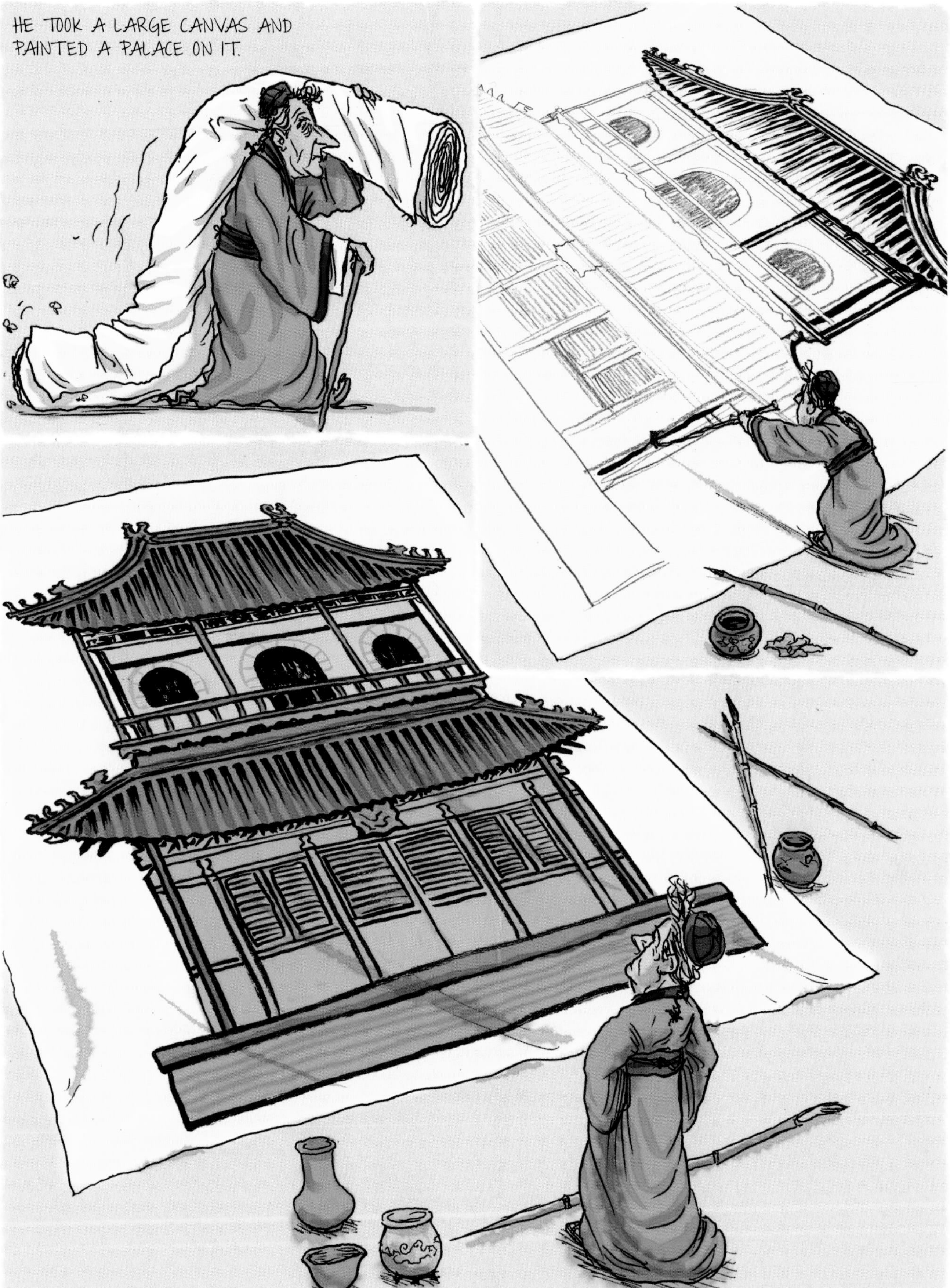
HE TOOK A LARGE CANVAS AND PAINTED A PALACE ON IT.
AND IT WAS PAINTED SO SKILLFULLY THAT IT LOOKED REAL.

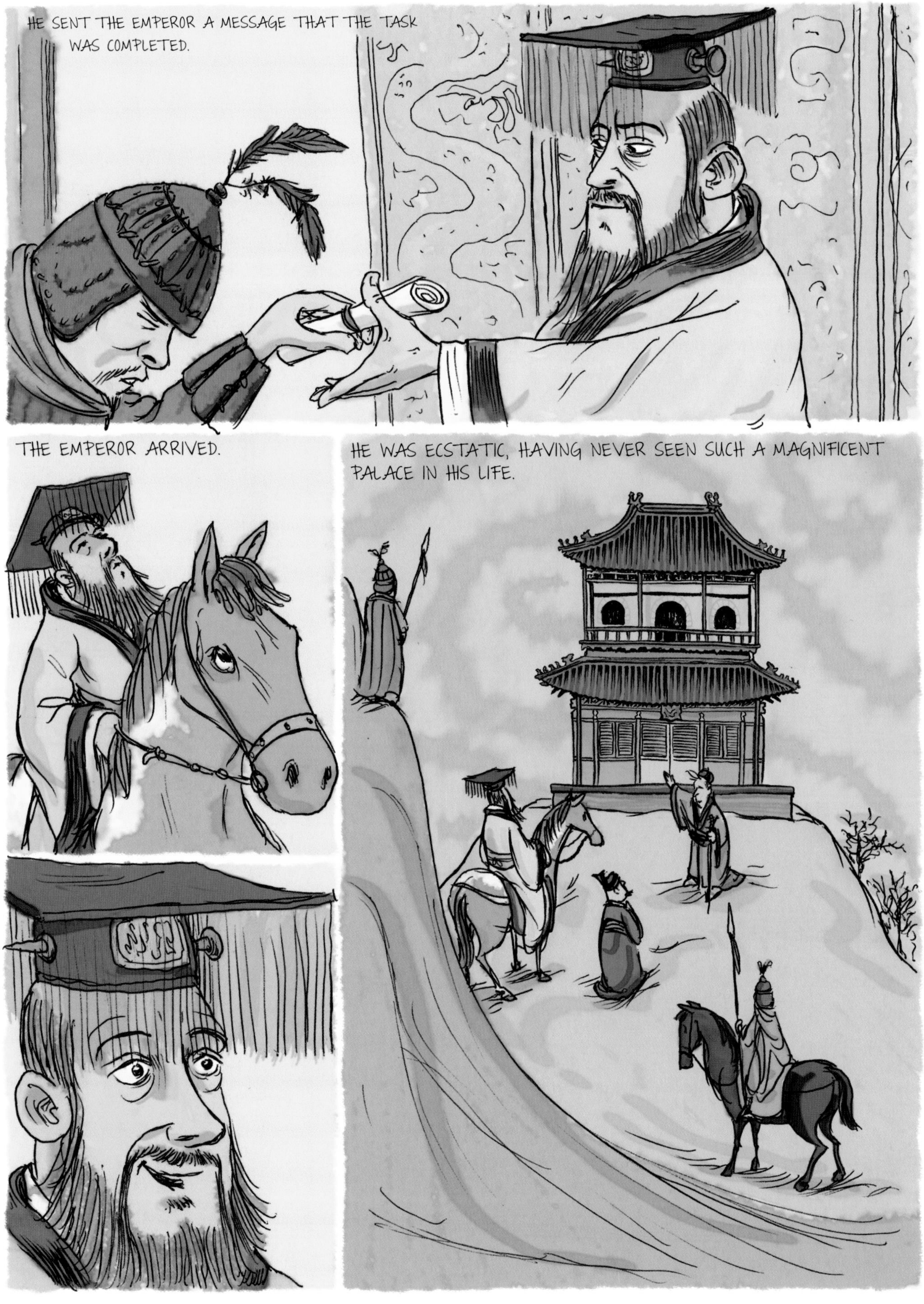
HE SENT THE EMPEROR A MESSAGE THAT THE TASK WAS COMPLETED.
THE EMPEROR ARRIVED.
HE WAS ECSTATIC, HAVING NEVER SEEN SUCH A MAGNIFICENT PALACE IN HIS LIFE.

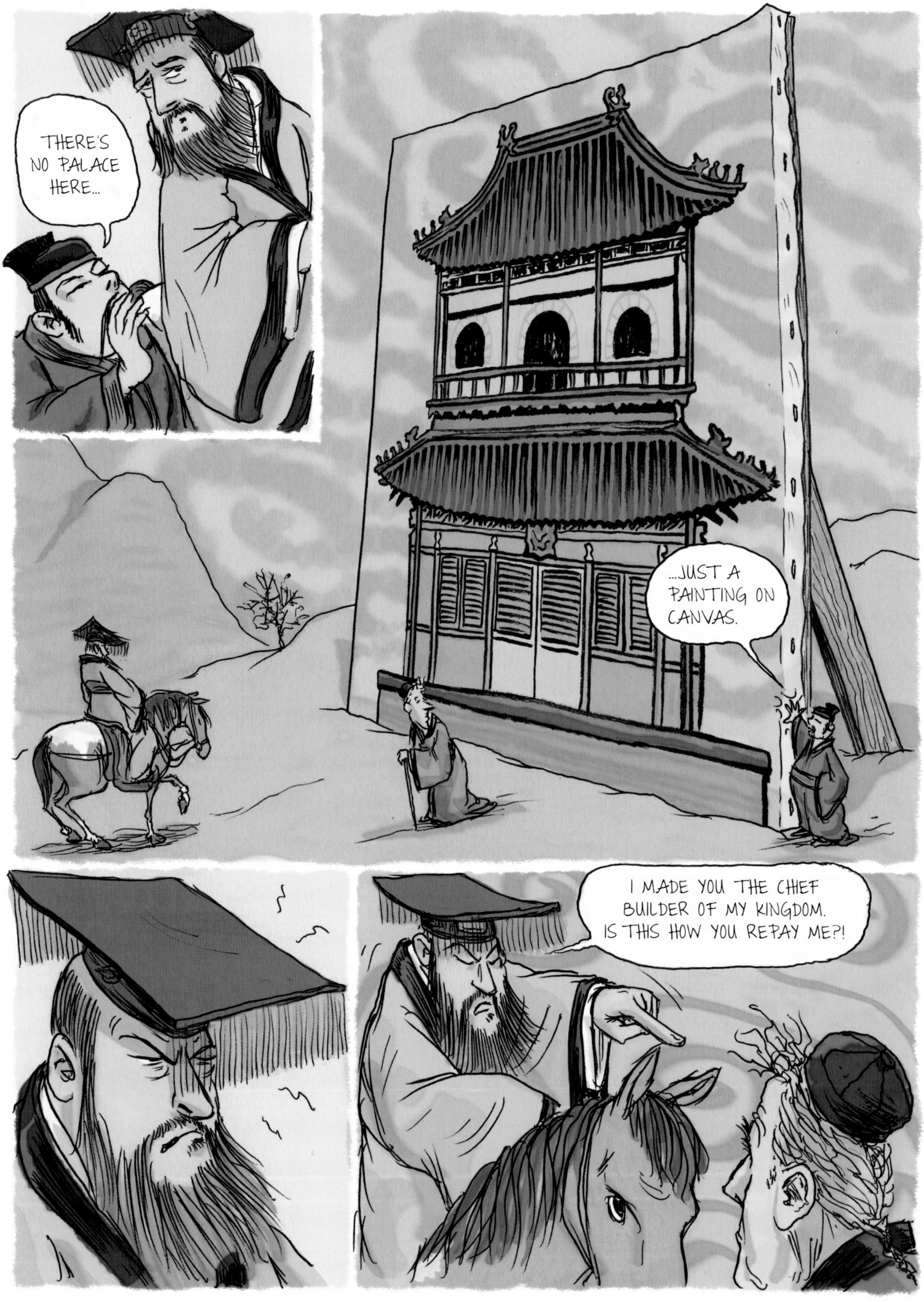
THERE'S NO PALACE HERE...
...JUST A PAINTING ON CANVAS.
I MADE YOU THE CHIEF BUILDER OF MY KINGDOM. IS THIS HOW YOU REPAY ME?!

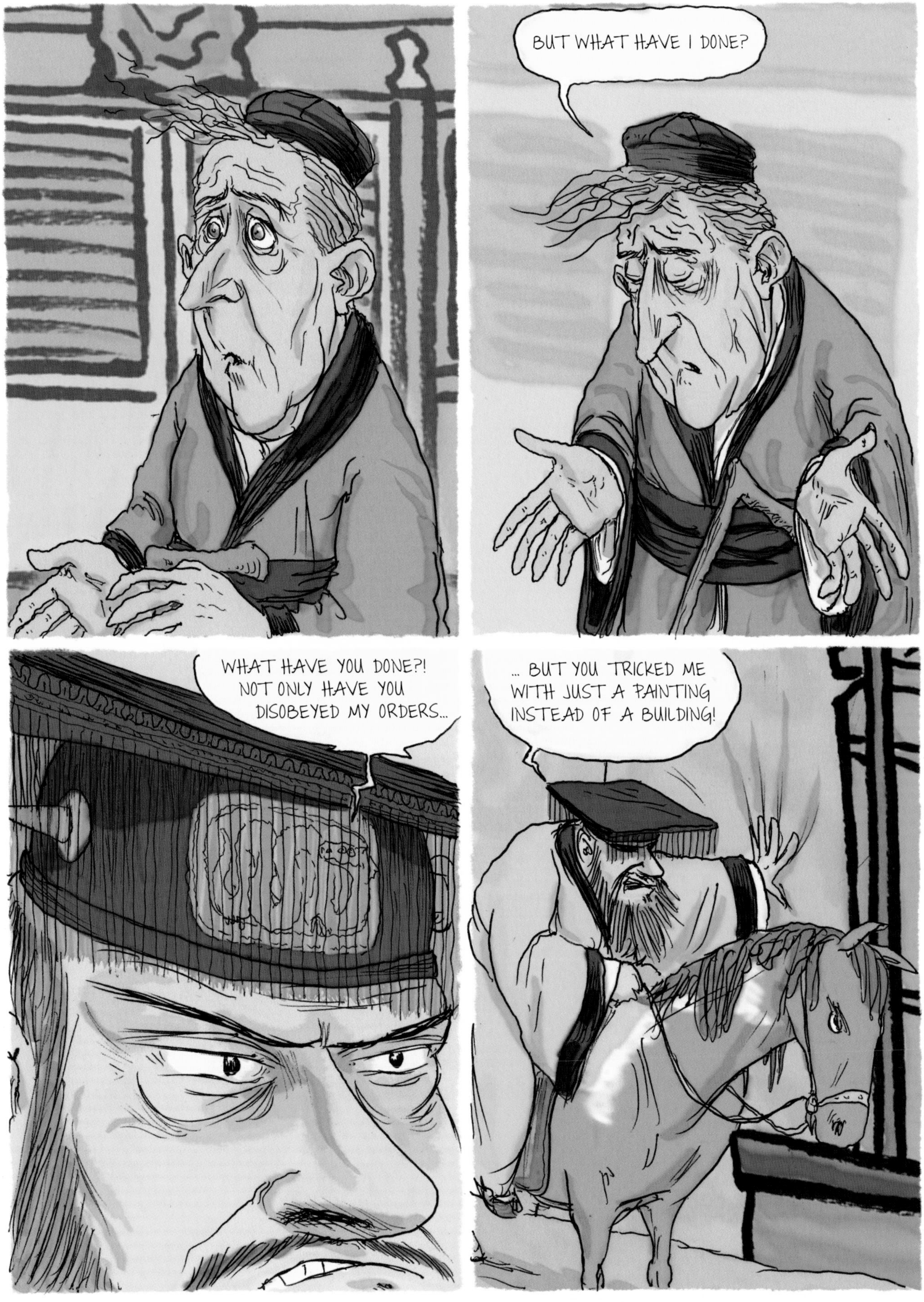
BUT WHAT HAVE I DONE?
WHAT HAVE YOU DONE?! NOT ONLY HAVE YOU DISOBEYED MY ORDERS...
... BUT YOU TRICKED ME WITH JUST A PAINTING INSTEAD OF A BUILDING!

JUST A PAINTING YOU SAY?

LET'S SEE.

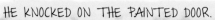
HE KNOCKED ON THE PAINTED DOOR.

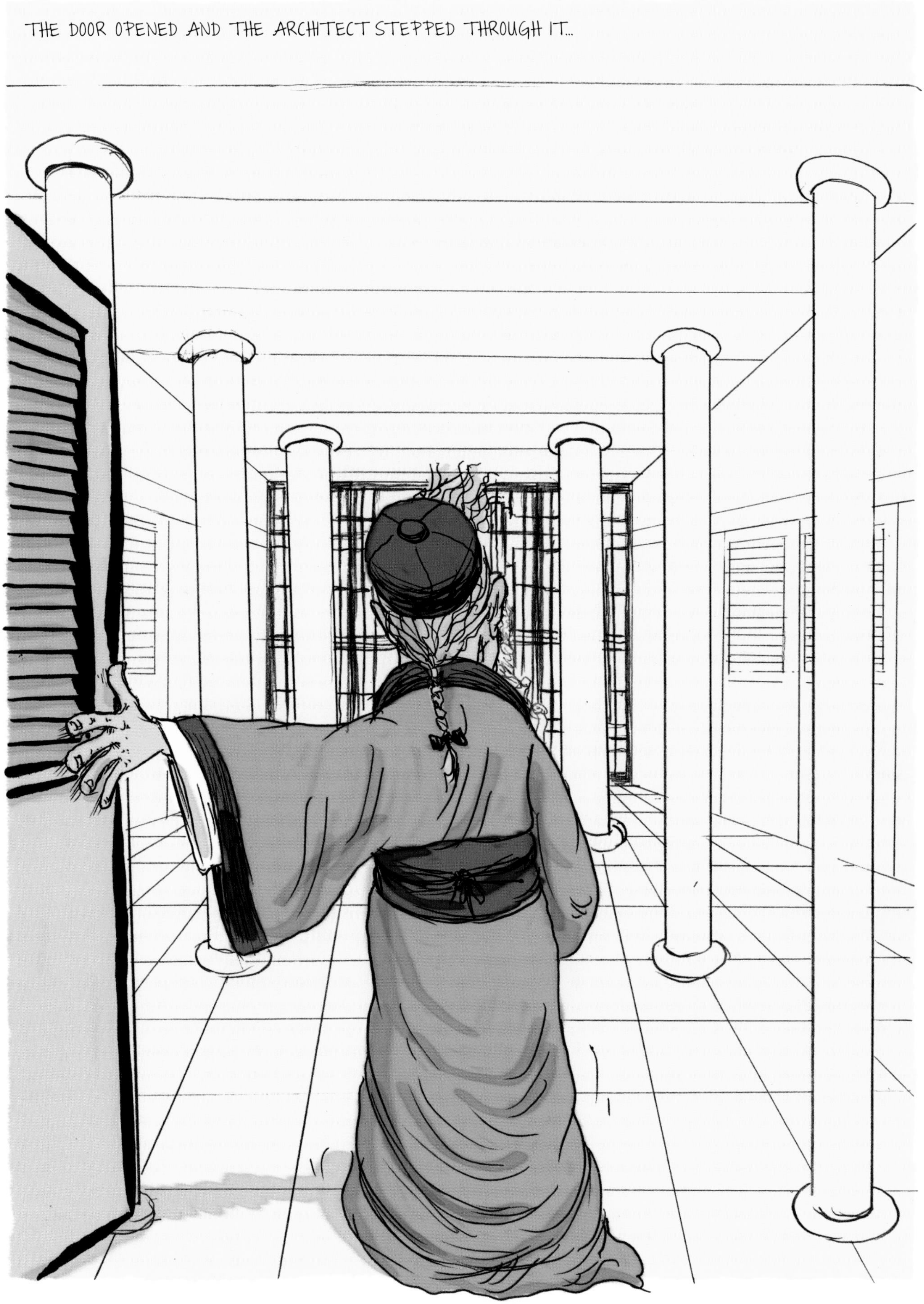
THE DOOR OPENED AND THE ARCHITECT STEPPED THROUGH IT...

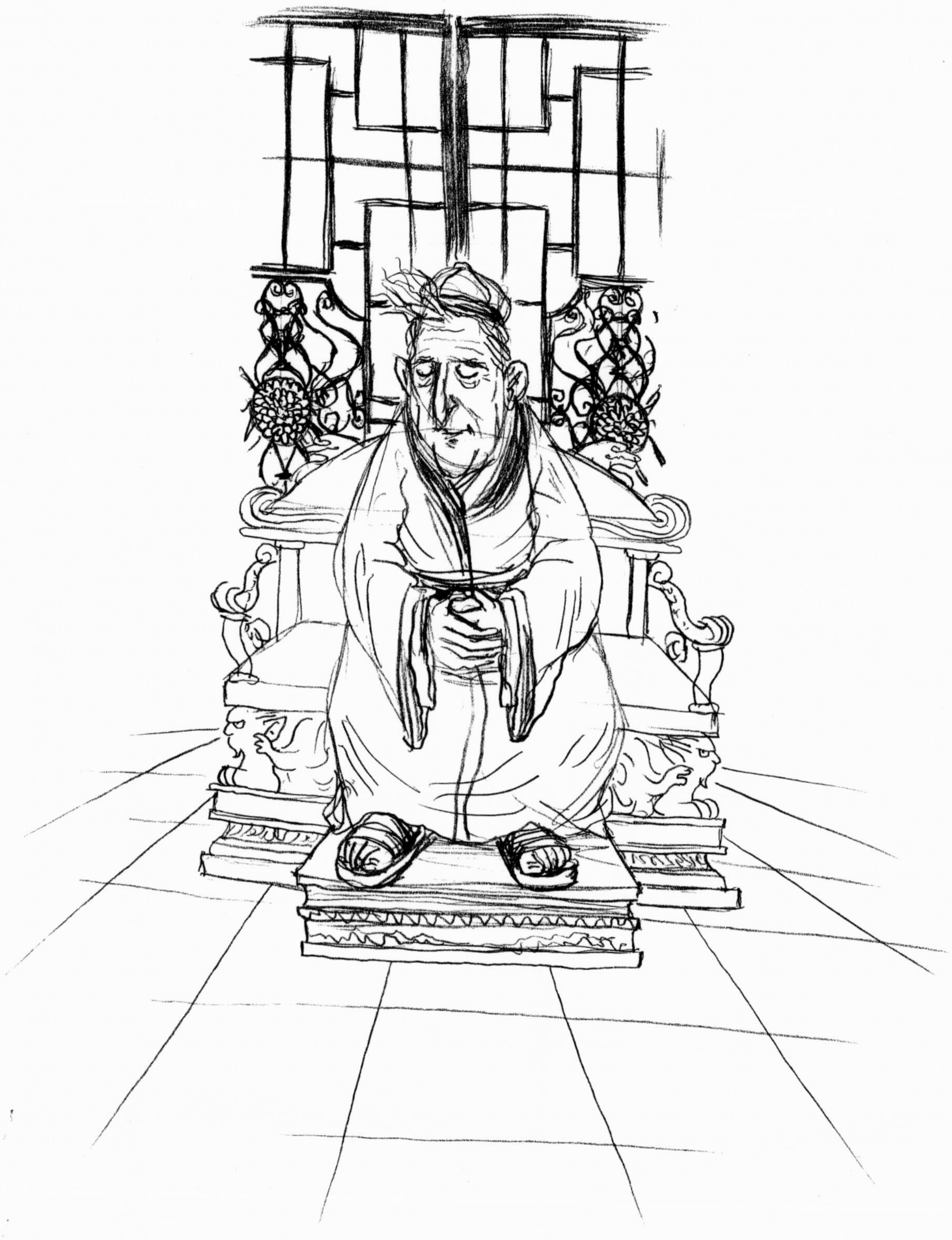

...AND NEVER LEFT AGAIN.